HOME JAMES

⬜⬜⬜⬜⬜⬜⬜⬜⬜⬜⬜⬜⬜⬜⬜⬜⬜⬜⬜⬜⬜⬜⬜⬜⬜⬜⬜⬜⬜⬜⬜⬜⬜

'What is your name?'
'James, Your Grace.'
'Christian name or surname?'
'Christian name, Your Grace.'
'I always call my servants by
their surnames. What is yours?'
'Darling, Your Grace.'
'Home, James.'

Lord Montagu of Beaulieu
and
Patrick Macnaghten

HOME JAMES

The Chauffeur in the Golden Age of Motoring

WEIDENFELD AND NICOLSON · LONDON

Contents

CONTENTS

Author's Note

Over a thousand chauffeurs, employers of chauffeurs, and descendants of both have contributed to the great fund of information upon which this book is based. It would be impossible to name them all, invidious to single any out, and I hope that they will all accept the deep gratitude which I offer as sincerely as if I were addressing each one individually.

Except where otherwise indicated, the illustrations have been provided by the Photographic Library of the National Motor Museum at Beaulieu, but many of these too were donated to the museum by former chauffeurs.

I am also particularly grateful to Barbara Cartland for her delightful Introduction, and to Philip Jenkinson, the well-known film historian, for the contents of Chapter 25.

From April 1980 to July 1981, my good friend and colleague Patrick Macnaghten and I were deeply involved in producing this book, based on preliminary classification and additional research by G. N. Georgano, then Chief Librarian of the National Motor Museum. In July 1981, Patrick and I had a meeting to check the final captions for the photographs in this book, and therefore I was most distressed to receive the news, only a few days later, of his untimely death, which brought to an end a career of writing for various media. I would like to pay special tribute to him for the skill with which he put this book together, and may it stand as a worthy memorial to Patrick's life-long interest in recording motoring history.

October 1981   Lord Montagu of Beaulieu

Introduction
by Barbara Cartland

As a great admirer of all Edward Montagu has done to arouse the public interest in cars of all ages, and being spellbound with admiration for his unique and brilliantly planned car museum at Beaulieu, I am thrilled to be asked to write the introduction for this, his new book.

The only qualification I have for such an honour is that I organized and drove in the first women's car race at Brooklands in 1931. It seems incredible today that I found enormous difficulty in finding women drivers.

Written up in the Press as 'the most remarkable race of the year', twelve competitors drove super-charged Midgets, the winner being Princess Averil Imeretinsky who was eventually to marry Ernest Simpson as his last wife.

It was my first experience of driving a car, and the only reason I got round the Brooklands course was that I was directed by Lord de Clifford, a well-known driver at the time – who later was to be the last peer to be tried by his peers in the House of Lords. I think this experience has made me, all my life, prefer to be driven rather than to drive myself.

In the war, as Chief Lady Welfare Officer of Bedfordshire, I was forced to drive for miles every day, seeking obscure search-light posts and secret ARP stations in a county from with every signpost had been removed in case they proved helpful to an invading enemy!

As I never had a lesson and never took a test, it really was a case of hit or miss – but I survived!

The one real difficulty was that for a long time I couldn't reverse, and had to find a convenient field in which to turn round when I wanted to go 'the other way'.

In the twenties I was driven by the dashing attractive and glamorous 'Bentley boys'. There was 'Babe' Barnato, a rich South African with beetle-black eyes, who won the Le Mans 24-hour race three years in succession, Tim Birkin, Jack Dunfee and of course, the fascinating Commander Glen Kidston, who was to lose his life piloting the ill-famed and unlucky aeroplane from which Alfred Lowenstein, the Belgian multi-millionaire and one of the super men of International Finance, fell to his death over the Channel.

I drove with the most popular motorist of the twenties, Dehane Segrave. A very attractive man with a lazy manner, he won the Grand Prix de France in 1923 and the world speed record in 1929 in his ice-cooled 1,000-horsepower Golden Arrow doing 231 miles per hour on Daytona Beach, Florida.

One evening when Dehane came to dinner, he had been summoned for driving slowly and causing an obstruction in Bond Street.

'I was looking at a very good pair of legs,' he laughed. Legs were still a novelty – a mini-skirt would have stopped the traffic!

When I arranged the first Charity Motor Rally at Bray, Malcolm Campbell helped me judge the exhibits. Malcolm, the son of a diamond merchant, achieved fantastic speeds, on land and sea. He raised the land speed record from 127 to 301 miles per hour, and the water speed from 74 to 141.

Naturally the most desirable 'chauffeur' of all is a young man who is in love. I have many memories of the early twenties, when it was a wild excitement to be able to drive away from chaperones and restrictions and the Social Church Parade in Hyde Park to 'pastures new'. The small hobbledehoy two-seater in which my young man drove me was very unreliable – punctures, lights which faded and slipping fanbelts were part of every expedition – but what fun it was!

One of the strangest and most difficult drivers I ever knew was Colonel George Henderson, a famous flying ace and the first pilot to fly under the Tower Bridge. His face had been burnt in the war and he was rather badly disfigured.

Because I was sorry for him he fell in love with me and followed me wherever I went, in an ugly open, noisy car he had constructed himself. He called it 'Barbed Arrow', a somewhat obscure play on my name, but

I found it very uncomfortable because it was just an engine covered with iron plate and mounted on a huge chassis, with two bucket seats from an aeroplane.

In 1930 George was the pilot in the tragic Meopham air disaster when the aeroplane fell to pieces in the air over Kent. It is one of the great flying mysteries which has never been solved because there was no explosion, the petrol tanks were intact, the cylinders uncracked. For the first time people talked of interference from 'outer space'.

Another friend, Commander Dennistoun Burney MP, a bluff blue-eyed sailor, invented the Burney Streamline Car. This had an engine at the back instead of the front, which was a revolutionary idea. It was, however, before the days of heating and the car was bitterly cold in the winter.

The Commander was thrilled when the Prince of Wales bought a Streamliner, but it had a most inconvenient habit of stalling. One day when the Prince was driving from Windsor the car stopped suddenly in the middle of the traffic on the outskirts of London.

'Its curious appearance,' the Prince said, 'attracted considerable attention, especially when the crowd saw I was inside it. Since it obstinately refused to start up again, I was obliged to send my driver to telephone for one of my other cars before I could continue my journey.'

The most intolerant chauffeurs in the world are those belonging to Maharajahs in India. These gorgeously turbaned men show their authority by tearing at a tremendous speed along the narrow strip of tarmacked road, invariably running over and scattering the precious grain which the peasants in the villages have spread out to dry.

Why, with miles and miles of untouched safe land, they must choose the road, only the Indians know, but as the car flashes by one hears the screams of protest and dismay fading into the dust.

The most dangerous drivers I have found anywhere are in Taiwan. The happy laughing Chinese drive at the fastest speed possible through densely crowded streets, while all the time turning their heads to talk animatedly to whoever is on the back seat. Every journey is spent in nerve-racking anticipation that the road behind will be strewn with corpses.

Sir Herbert Austin, whom I knew well because the Austin works were in my brother's parliamentary constituency, told me:

'I sketched it on the billiard table at home. I was determined to produce a car which would be stored in the side entrance of any ordinary suburban villa and could carry four passengers.' He succeeded in 1922, and the

Austin Seven cost only £165. Compare that with the price of the Mini today!

I had my first car ride when I was five in 1906. It seemed to me that I flew on the wings of angels! Crossing the Atlantic this year in Concorde at over 1300 miles per hour – twice the speed of sound – to arrive in New York before we had left England, I wondered where such progress will lead us. Will we eventually die before we are born? Who knows? And it all started with the man who invented the wheel.

Chuff Chuff

The Castle of Mey, owned and restored by Her Majesty Queen Elizabeth the Queen Mother, stands remote and tranquil on the northernmost coast of Scotland. But one August day the peace of the place was disrupted. Borne gently on the breeze there came an unfamiliar sound. At first a distant rumble like faraway thunder, it drew closer and the air was filled with a rhythmic throbbing. It became more insistent, more compelling.

Windows at the castle opened, and one by one heads popped out. But among them was not that of Her Majesty, for a full century was to pass before she came to reside at the Castle of Mey. For this was the year 1860.

The rumbling grew louder, and the eager listeners could distinguish the individual notes which made up the cacophony of discord. There was a chugging and a chuffing, a rattling and a roaring. They waited, agog. The tension was almost unbearable.

Then, a long way off, across the flat countryside they could see a puff of something. Dust? Smoke? Steam? As it drew slowly closer they could make out something solid in the midst of the moving cloud. They could even see some details now. There was a big round barrel with a chimney sticking out of the top, and wheels as big as a cart's, and three people, a woman and two men, sitting in a row. The strange apparition moved inexorably towards the astonished onlookers, and the more fanciful of them thought it resembled nothing so much as a carriage jolting along without a horse, if such a thing could be.

The contraption came right up to the castle and drew to a halt at the very entrance. It stood there, wheezing and quivering like an asthmatic racehorse. One of the men climbed stiffly to the ground and then turned to hand down the woman. The Earl and Countess of Caithness had ridden home in triumph.

And triumph it certainly was. For this was no showman's stunt. It was a practical demonstration of the theories which Lord Caithness had propounded to the British Association for the Advancement of Science at a meeting at Oxford two years earlier. He was a rich man with a lively mind, a worthy descendant of the eighteenth-century tradition of aristocrats carrying out scientific experiments in elegant laboratories set up in their stately homes. He commissioned his steam carriage from a small firm which made agricultural machinery, the Castle Foundry at Buckingham.

Small though it was, the vehicle required a two-man crew, one to steer and one to stoke. For the long drive from Inverness, whither the carriage had been sent by sea, Lord Caithness guided the machine himself, while crouched on the rear platform feverishly shovelling coal into the firebox, was the manager of the Castle Foundry, Thomas Rickett.

The fourth member of the party was the Reverend William Ross, of Kintore, who had literally come along for the ride.

It is a hundred and forty-six miles from Inverness to the Castle of Mey, and the road rises nine hundred feet to cross a mountain known as the Ord of Caithness. It is a nine-mile climb and involves gradients as steep as 1 in 7. But under the Earl's determined hand, and with Thomas Rickett desperately stoking, the little machine doggedly chugged its way to the top.

But a civic reception was awaiting the party at Wick and Lord Caithness was not stretching his luck. He prudently enlisted the aid of horses to drag the steamer to the top of the next obstacle, Berriedale. This lack of confidence put Thomas Rickett on his mettle, so he wielded his shovel more energetically than ever, and they trundled into Wick in fine style at a spanking eighteen miles per hour.

As if the merry rattling and snorting was not already noise enough, the dignitaries of the town arranged for a cannon to be fired to announce the Earl's arrival. They thereupon created him an honorary burgess of Wick. In acknowledging the honour, Lady Caithness proclaimed that its bestowal on her husband made that one of the proudest and happiest days of her life. In an outburst of chauvinistic hyperbole she exulted in the fact that he, a Caithness man, had shown the doubters in the South that it was possible for a steam carriage to cross the Ord of Caithness, a feat which they had deemed impossible. It is not clear whether by 'South' she meant Oxford, where the members of the British Association had expressed polite disbelief in the Earl's claims, or Edinburgh, which people from her part of the world are still apt to regard as pretty near the Equator.

But however much the good people of Wick allowed themselves to be carried away by what they regarded as a purely local achievement, the fact remains that the vehicle itself, no less than the figure huddled on its platform, hailed from Buckinghamshire.

However it was neither placid Buckinghamshire nor wild Caithness which was destined to be the cradle of what Lord Caithness called 'Road Locomotion'. Although in the next twenty years steam carriages appeared at the rate of one a year, they never really caught on, and when the commercial breakthrough came, a generation after Lord Caithness's epic journey, it was made by the internal rather than the external combustion engine. Steam locomotives flourished on the railways, but their development off the tracks was confined to traction engines and the rolling of roads for other vehicles to drive on.

The Motor Age dawned, not in Britain at all, but on the Continent of Europe. It was in 1894 that the Hon. Evelyn Ellis bought a Panhard in France, before shipping it to England the following year. This 53-year-old man was not in good health, and when he planned an ambitious tour of the Continent he did not feel up to doing the driving himself. Lord Caithness had formed half of his own two-man team but, as Evelyn Ellis was not going to take part, if he were to follow the formula he would need to employ both a mechanic and a driver. This seemed to weight the ratio of crew to passenger absurdly in favour of the hired help. So Evelyn Ellis decided to take the bold step of dispensing with the services of a skilled engineer. Instead, he employed a driver and sent him for a six-week course at the Panhard works. Obviously he could not expect to obtain a man with the knowledge of a Thomas Rickett, but this driver seems to have been wholly without previous experience.

However, Evelyn Ellis's courageous experiment turned out a total success. 'Though he has never had any other mechanical training he has been everything I could require,' he wrote of his driver at the end of the long tour which lasted for several weeks and which entailed traversing France from south to north, from Marseilles to Le Havre. Commenting on his experience with a driver who had only had a limited technical training Ellis was convinced that high engineering skill was not necessary, and that a bright man who had mastered the rudiments could perfectly well be given charge of a motor car.

'Now if this is possible in France,' Ellis wrote, 'surely the average English coachman has enough intelligence to do the same, and would find no difficulty in adapting himself to the new order of things when this method of locomotion becomes more common.'

'Method of locomotion' seems a pretty clumsy way of describing motoring, but these pioneers had not yet had time to work out a vocabulary. When they did they largely adopted French words –*chassis, tonneau, cabriolet*, and so forth. But the early work of Thomas Rickett and his like was not entirely forgotten. Although petrol engines need no coal, the man who performed the job which superseded the role of stoker was still known as the 'fireman'. Naturally, though, it was the French version of the word which was used – *chauffeur*.

2

'They Order, Said I, This Matter Better in France'

Laurence Sterne

To Evelyn Ellis's rhetorical question, 'Now if this is possible in France surely the average English coachman has enough intelligence to do the same, and would find no difficulty in adapting himself to the new order of things?' the answer must be a reluctant 'Well, no.'

The English coachman may have had the intelligence, but the difficulty of adapting himself seems to have been insuperable. There were two reasons for this. Firstly the new 'method of locomotion' was considerably more advanced on the Continent of Europe than in Britain, and consequently there had been time for it to attract away from the horses the sort of men who would be interested in it. The second reason why established coachmen were not suitable was that they were deeply steeped in the tradition of their craft and reluctant to attempt the mental somersault required to adopt a completely different one.

The coachman was a respected figure with a history interwoven into legend, not only in England but across the world. There were many pulse-quickening stories of heroic coachmen fighting off attackers and protecting their terrified passengers against anything from wolves slavering at the panic-stricken horses drawing sleighs through the snowbound forests of Russia and Poland, to marauding Red Indians in the Middle West of the United States. Legion, too, were the tales of gallant coachmen tackling the most heavily-armed and determined highwaymen.

As well as these stirring tales there were also many lighter anecdotes, handed down through the centuries. For instance, in the village of Milton Abbas in Dorset they were still recalling, at the beginning of the

Motor Age, an incident which had taken place a hundred and fifty years before. It concerned the coachman to the landowner who had built the model village and housed in it all the inhabitants of the old cottages which he had submerged under a sheet of ornamental water. The inhabitants had not been consulted in the matter and by no means all of them took kindly to it. It was, therefore, through an atmosphere of smouldering discontent that the lord of the manor drove up the trim new village street on the first stage of his journey to London.

At the top of the hill the equipage suffered some minor mishap, the eighteenth-century equivalent of a puncture. It was not serious but it necessitated a stop for the coachman to carry out repairs. While he was doing whatever it was, the stillness of the afternoon was shattered by a joyous peal of bells from the church tower. The landowner enquired of the coachman why the bells were being rung.

'Ah, my lord,' replied the coachman with devastating candour, 'they always ring the bells in celebration whenever you go away.'

Even today the people of Milton Abbas will recount this story to explain why the bells were arbitrarily removed, so that the tower remained silent for many years. The tale of the wicked landowner and the stupid coachman is told with indignation or amusement depending upon the social attitude of the teller.

A rather happier tale of a coachman – and a village – steeped in the old tradition comes from Stoke Edith in Herefordshire. When the lady of the manor was expected back from a journey, a man was stationed in the church tower to spy out the carriage as it breasted the hill on the horizon. He would tell the bell-ringers, so that as the carriage reached the village it was greeted with a merry peal. This happened not in the remote past but almost within living memory, for it was recalled by a gardener employed there who died in 1957, aged eighty-eight.

Small wonder, then, that coachmen, heirs to a heritage running back through hundreds of years in the folklore of their country, did not leap at the opportunity of embarking on a completely new and different life. It might be all right for a young groom or stable lad to chance his arm with these new-fangled contraptions, but it was far beneath the dignity of a full-blown head coachman. Serene and confident on his box, looking out along the backs of his sleek horses, controlling the whole magnificent turn-out with a subtle flick of the wrists, the coachman enjoyed a delicious sense of power and importance. Who would surrender all that in exchange for the worries and horrors of trundling along behind a lot of exploding gas? And, worse, what if the gas stopped exploding? The coachman would not have the faintest idea what to do.

A coachman's duty was not confined to driving. In a big establishment he would be in charge of a large number of servants divided into groups of 'stable servants', 'riding servants', and 'driving servants'. As well as driving his employers on the more important occasions he was responsible for seeing that the grooms kept the horses properly fed, cleaned, and turned out. Besides all this he had to order from and approve the bills of the corn merchant, the coachbuilder, the saddler, the horsedealer, and the tailor who supplied the liveries. Above all, he often held the ultimate sanction of hiring and firing the other stable servants. With all this accumulated power many coachmen turned into benevolent autocrats with a happy band of eager helpers. Others became petty tyrants, loathed by their underlings and obstinately obstructing their employers' wishes.

In 1874 there was published *The Book of the Horse*, and in it the author, S. Sidney, recorded that 'in the great studs of easy-going noblemen one has known instances where "my lord" has not been permitted to go into the stables without the stud-groom's permission, or to select any particular horse for his own riding, or to drive out on days or at hours not agreeable to the body coachman' ('body coachman' was an alternative name for 'head coachman'). It is hardly possible to imagine that, a mere twenty years later, the same nobleman would be likely to go into the stableyard and say to the resident dictator, 'Oh, by the way, I'm scrapping all this and buying a motor. You'll have to drive it.'

If the poor man was misguided enough to want to change the age-old order, his best course was to introduce, with the car, a man from its country of origin, whose English was not good enough for him to understand what the other servants were saying about him.

The problems with coachmen were not confined to the British Isles. Francis Underhill published his *Driving for Pleasure* in New York in 1896, and in it remarked that in all America he doubted whether there were twenty-five men who could rightly be called head or body coachmen. He then proceeded to list the qualifications and the method of their attainment. This started with the boyhood job of exerciser ('he is taught to walk smartly, and not with the slouching step of the plowboy, and how to put a certain snap into his work'), followed by that of tiger (originally a page who rode on a platform behind a carriage). After working as a carriage groom the young man would progress to the driving of first a single horse, then a pair, before ultimately winning through to the driving of a tandem or four-in-hand.

Underhill ended his blue-print of the perfect head coachman with the words, 'and finally he must not use liquor to excess'. In those days drink problems were hardly problems at all. With little traffic, and what there was moving slowly, the risk of accident was slight, and providing nothing got broken employers were not all that strict. Even Queen Victoria took a tolerant view of drunken servants on special occasions. Farmers on their way back from market were notorious for letting the horse jog along while they had a refreshing nap in the trap. 'The old mare knows her way home,' was a remark often heard.

There was, of course, some excuse for coachmen fortifying themselves against a long drive on a cold night for, perched up on the box, they had no protection from the weather. But there is the story of one who overdid it. When his employer emerged from the house where he had been dining, his coachman was fast asleep. He was so drunk that all efforts to wake him failed. Finally, with the assistance of bystanders, the employer laid him out on the floor of the carriage and himself clambered up on to the box to drive home.

It was quite a long way and there was frost in the air, so he was thankful to turn in through the gates and up the long avenue. At last the house came into view, discreet shafts of light escaping from between the thick curtains of its many windows. It looked warm and welcoming, and he pictured the roaring fire in the library and the hot toddy brought by his solicitous butler. For this was a smoothly run house which prided itself on doing things properly. They even had a drill for opening the front door. The hall-boy would be stationed at a window in the hall to keep watch for the oil lamps of the carriage as it breasted the rise in the avenue. He would alert the footman who would inform the butler who would, if not exactly spring into action, roll forward with that gliding motion reminiscent of a train drawing away from a platform. He would open the door and descend the steps, timing his arrival at the bottom to coincide with the precise moment that the carriage drew up, so that as the wheels stopped turning he could grasp the handle and swing open the door while the footman stood by to lower the steps.

So it was on this night. But there were no lights on the outside of the house, and the interior of the carriage was in darkness. All the butler could see was that the seat was empty. The recumbent figure on the floor lay in deepest shadow.

The butler was taken aback. Puzzled, he addressed the dim figure huddled on the box. In the butler's voice there was more curiosity than concern, as he enquired, 'What have you done with the old bugger, then?'

3

The Last of the Old

When one considers how firmly established in English life was the horse and everything and everyone to do with it, it is quite astonishing that the motor car ever got its bonnet in at all. That it did is a tribute to the determination of the scientifically-minded pioneers, among whom must be numbered the first chauffeurs.

These early motorists were on a very sticky wicket indeed. They were not just cranks covering themselves with oil in the woodshed, they demanded that their nasty machines should be accommodated in the very temple of equestrian transport, the well-ventilated coach-house. The gleaming elegant broughams and victorias had to be pushed out of the way and, to make it worse, these disgusting motors were not above making puddles on the shining tiles of the floor.

Not content with raising havoc in their own stableyards, these selfish, insensitive madmen ventured out to make themselves a nuisance on the public highway. You never knew when you might round a corner to find the lane blocked by one of these snorting quivering monsters with, seated at the tiller, a figure in a fur coat, wearing its cap on back to front, and its red-rimmed eyes staring out through sinister goggles. It was indeed an apparition to frighten the horses, and frighten the horses it did. And even when it was silent, broken down at the roadside with the occupants crawling underneath it like worms beneath a stone, the sight was still bizarre enough to send the most stolid pony leaping into the hedge and attempting to pull the dogcart up after it.

Unless you just happened to be the sort of lunatic to whom motoring made an instant, irresistible appeal, you were not likely to want to have anything to do with the beastly smelly things. Of course the very last people to offer themselves for conversion were those high priests of the cult of the horse, head coachmen.

The owner, or prospective owner, of a motor car had to look elsewhere for somebody to manage it for him. While the earliest cars were quite easy to equip with a chauffeur from their country of origin, once cars began to be manufactured in England the supply of foreigners was not enough to meet the demand, and chauffeurs – or rather men capable of becoming chauffeurs – had to be sought nearer home. It was not easy to find men with both the necessary skills and the adventurous spirit required, and the least promising place in which to look was the servants' hall. Nevertheless, it was to the servants' hall that many early car owners turned. The reason was that the servant class or tribe was so large and formed such an important part of the social structure that it was natural for a private employer to search there first, rather than venture outside it.

Some idea of the social structure at the dawn of the Motor Age can be deduced from figures taken from the survey of England and Wales made in 1891. Of a total population of twenty-nine million, domestic servants accounted for just under two million, whereas under the heading 'Professional' appeared a figure of less than one million. Presumably this included not merely the Church, and the medical and legal professions, but all the officers of the Army and Navy. 'Commercial' and 'Agricultural and Fishing' totalled 1·3 million each, while under the heading 'Industrial' appeared 25·3% of the population, or 7·3 million. By far the largest category of all, however, was 'Children and Unoccupied Adults', who made up no less than 55·5% of the population and numbered comfortably over sixteen million. Obviously the number of children included must have been considerable, but even so the amount of 'Unoccupied' is still very high. 'Unoccupied' was the most delicate of all euphemisms for 'unemployed', but it was, for the most part, voluntary unemployment. As the Rt. Hon. Harold Macmillan was to say half a century later, 'There is nothing wrong with unemployment as such. If you've got enough money you call it "leisure".' It was from the ranks of the 'Unoccupied' that the pioneer motorists sprang, and they had, by definition, almost unlimited time to spend on their new hobby. However, just as they employed grooms to look after their hunters, so they employed chauffeurs to look after their cars. And, just as the hunters were ridden by the owners, so the cars were driven by them, with the chauffeur acting as 'riding mechanic' ready to repair a puncture or crawl under the car to see to one of the mysterious ills that early machinery was heir to.

It was, of course, essential that the chauffeur should have had some training, preferably at the factory where the car was made. Most owners realized this, but they did not necessarily appreciate that the man should be one who had some aptitude for work. Into the round hole of the driving seat many square pegs were uncomfortably jammed. These were mostly men of middle-age or older, who found the new skills impossible to acquire. On the other hand, the more sensible owners chose young men with natural mechanical ability and sent them off to the factory for a few months before the car was delivered.

The majority of early chauffeurs started life as servants in some other capacity. Employers looking for a man to be trained as a chauffeur tended to select one from their own staff. There were two main reasons for this. The coming of the car would probably make a groom or stableboy redundant, and employers on the whole were reluctant to make him unemployed – that is, to join the unmoneyed section of the 'Unoccupied'. Secondly, he was already a trained servant, used to the ways of the household. For the sake of peace in the servants' hall this was extremely important.

Domestic service was regarded as a career, and progress in it was marked by clearly defined privileges. An elaborate and rigid protocol had grown up with long usage and, at least in the larger establishments, was strictly adhered to. All the servants would breakfast together, because most of the day's work was fitted into the morning and there was no time for dignified ritual. But luncheon and dinner were ceremonial occasions when the full process was enacted in smooth solemnity. The senior servants graced the 'hall' table for the first course and in some cases they enforced a rule of silence. At a signal from the housekeeper they would rise and make their stately withdrawal to the housekeeper's room, where they would finish their meal, far from the disturbing giggles of house-maids and the chaffing of footmen. In some houses the upper servants took their puddings with them; in the grander ones they had a footman to wait upon them.

Rather than try to import a new member into this mannered arabesque, many pioneer motorists preferred not to risk upsetting the whole powerful body of servant opinion and therefore settled for a likely lad already in their employ. Though few can have been as thorough about it as the Devonshire landowner who chose one of his young grooms who had joined the establishment as stableboy at the age of nine. He was sent to the Daimler factory where he served a full apprenticeship. In due course, bearing his indentures and a certificate warranting that he was a fully-trained Daimler mechanic he proudly drove home the car which his employer had ordered. It was one of the first to be seen in Devon, and it aroused enormous interest, with the chauffeur playing something of the role of the keeper of a performing bear. But his employer had not finished yet. With his single-minded approach to the whole serious business of motoring he would not leave the job half done.

Everything had worked out well so far. The right boy had been chosen and had acquired the necessary qualifications entirely according to plan. The motor had been selected after considerable thought, carefully weighing its advantages and disadvantages against those of other makes. It had been built according to instructions and now, at last, here it was. It was time to embark on the second part of the meticulously conceived scheme. The car must be tested. If it should be found capable of performing its function, well and good. If not, it would be disposed of and the young chauffeur would resume his interrupted career in the stables. Everything depended on the test. Man and machine must demonstrate that they could acquit themselves with honour.

With a man like that testing a motor car was not, as it was with lesser mortals, a matter of seeing whether the thing could climb the nearest hill and, if so, turn round at the top and stop at the bottom on the way home. Nothing less than traversing the country literally from end to end would do. Accordingly the vehicle was shipped to John o' Groats and driven down through Scotland and England as far as the Devon estate. But it did not end there. A test was a test, and it must be completed properly or it was no good at all. On they went, right down to Land's End. Then and only then, after a journey of nine hundred miles which had taken two weeks, was the owner satisfied that this remarkable new outfit was worthy of a place in his heated and well-ventilated motor house.

Although this particular car-owner had the best of both worlds – trained servant and trained mechanic – others were content to hand the new task over to the coachman and hope for the best. Lurid tales are told of these men treating cars like horses, flapping their elbows when they came to hump-backed bridges, saying 'Whoa!' when they wanted to stop, or making encouraging clicking noises in the hope that a broken-down engine would respond in the way which you would take for granted with any self-respecting horse.

Many coachmen, did of course, end up as perfectly adequate chauffeurs, but they were the exceptions. Apart from the mental attitude, there was the question of age. Young men are always more eager to tackle new things than their elders – already set in their ways – and the majority of coachmen were at least of middle age. Chauffeuring was, they felt, better left to the youngsters.

One can certainly not imagine a coachman performing the task which Jack Stephens accomplished in 1899. He accompanied the second Lord Montagu as riding mechanic in the Paris–Ostend race, in the first British-made car driven by an Englishman to race on the Continent. This was no sinecure, as he had to lie along the mudguard striking matches to keep the hot-tube ignition alight. They came third.

The first of the Beaulieu chauffeurs, his early indoctrination into racing gave him a taste for speed and, as he was also a remarkably fearless man, he became a terrifyingly reckless driver. After two cars had come to a disastrous end at his hands, it was mutually decided that he would be better employed doing something less expensive, and he went off and became a woodman, to be succeeded by his brother.

At the end of the nineteenth century and the beginning of the twentieth the motor car was very much an unknown quantity and its future speculative. At best it was an intriguing toy, at worst a squalid nuisance. A man had to be adventurous indeed to hitch his star to a wagon so likely to backfire.

One such adventurous spirit was a Scot named Peter Robertson, a man in his late twenties in the very early years of the twentieth century. He owned a little bicycle shop in Blairgowrie, where his talent for engineering had but limited scope. For he was richly endowed with the hands and mind of an engineer like so many of his countrymen who found fulfillment in the engine-rooms of ships or locomotive workshops all over the world. But Peter had never been out of Perthshire.

He had read about motor cars, he had seen pictures of motor cars, but until one day in 1902 he had never actually encountered one. When he did it was stationary, broken down at the roadside. From beneath it protruded the legs of two young men. In the tonneau sat their father, comfortably leaning back at his ease with his hat tipped over his eyes and his labrador on the seat beside him.

Peter dismounted from his bicycle and stood watching, his glance running over the car from its single central headlight to the tips of its rear mudguards. The gentleman in the tonneau beckoned him over.

'Do you know anything about these things?' he enquired.

Peter conceded that this was the first car he had seen, but claimed to know something of machinery. At this point one of the young men wriggled out from under, holding in his hand two pieces of metal rod.

'Sheered right off, I don't know where the hell we're going to get another one. Have to send to Coventry, I suppose.'

Peter stretched out his hand. 'Likely I can weld it,' he said. 'I've a wee workbench in Blairgowrie.'

In a very short time he was back, caressing the repaired rod as lovingly as a woman caresses a fur.

'May I see?' The gentleman in the tonneau held out his hand and turned the rod round, inspecting the weld. 'A beautiful job,' he pronounced. Then he directed a shrewd and piercing look at Peter. 'Would you like a job as a chauffeur?' he enquired.

Peter was a man of few words. 'Aye,' he replied.

Thus began an association which continued, through good times and bad, until Peter reached the age of sixty-five just before the Second World War.

The immediate recruitment of an engineer within an hour or two of him seeing a car for the first time may have been unusual, but the engagement of a chauffeur at first meeting was not. Any company which delivered a car to a new owner risked losing the driver. As one autocratic customer declared, 'I'll only buy the car if I can have the man with it. Both or neither.'

Peter Robertson's career was typical of many which started in those placid settled Edwardian days. It was not long before cars crossed a new threshold of reliability and in doing so extended enormously the scope of feasible travel by road. It soon became clear that the motor car had come to stay. And as long as there were cars, so there would be chauffeurs needed to look after them. With no hint of war to cast a shadow over the distant horizon a young man could plan an interesting future away from the factory bench, the wheelbarrow, or the stable tack room.

Exactly how these eager young men were going to fit themselves into the ordered scheme of the traditional household, with all its rules and customs and long-established traditions, was a problem which was to exercise the patience and ingenuity of employers and employees alike for many years to come.

4

The First of the New

In the first five years of the twentieth century the number of cars in Britain rose from 1,000 to 8,400 and in the United States from 8,000 to 79,000. Cars did not come automatically equipped with chauffeurs, but many – probably the great majority – of the owners required help to keep the cars on the road, or indeed to keep them at all. The recruitment of these helpers may have been done unimaginatively, as in the case of the employer who stated firmly, 'the man who drives my 'osses is the only man who is going to be allowed to drive my motor', or haphazardly like Peter Robertson, but once appointed they all became chauffeurs.

What nobody was very clear about was what the term 'chauffeur' actually embraced. As it was succintly put in *The Chauffeur's Blue Book*, a publication which appeared in 1906 from the pen of one coyly describing himself as 'a well-known chauffeur', 'We chauffeurs, you know, are a class and type of men that have never existed before. There are no recognized customs and rules of our order. We have not been brought up to our work, and we have nobody to guide our general conduct.'

The great gulf between those chauffeurs who switched from one department of domestic service to another and those who came from the factory was in the matter of hours worked. Servants were accustomed to being on call when needed; factory workers were used to clocking off and going home at the end of the shift. The mechanically-minded men from the workbench undoubtedly serviced the cars better, but the employers were better served by men who had trained as servants.

The correspondence pages of *The Autocar* were kept well supplied with complaints about chauffeurs in the first decade of the century. 'The slackness of my chauffeur is a daily trial,' bleated one employer. One wonders why he tolerated this irritation until one reads the next sentence: 'Not that he fails in competence, far from it.' That was the rub. Either you put up with impertinence, real or imagined, and had your car efficiently serviced and driven by 'a class and type of men that have never existed before', or you spent hours sitting at the roadside hoping that someone would come along and tell your perfectly-behaved coachman what to do. 'His manners! Ye gods, how my grooms would stare at him!' continued the same correspondent.

Most people introduced motoring gradually. They did not immediately sell all their horses and carriages and dismiss their grooms and coachmen, and consequently there existed an uneasy dichotomy. In the stableyard there was often open hostility. The men who had devoted their lives to the horse felt that not only their jobs but the whole purpose of their orderly existence was threatened. The brash young chauffeurs agreed that they and their way of life did indeed pose a threat – and, they added, a jolly good thing too. They reacted with derision towards the disciplines, customs and standards which tradition had hallowed. They stubbornly refused to accept that the old ways had anything to recommend them and they were determined not to conform. It did not occur to them that the last of the old is nearly always better than the first of the new.

To a young man with his head full of modern technological marvels like sprags and sprockets and trembler coils it must have been intensely irritating to spend so long in the company of coachmen and grooms who had nothing better to do than devote their attention to the cleanliness of their charges. All very well for them to spend hours polishing a carriage. It had only a body to bother about. If the motor was the same he would probably not mind rubbing away at it himself. But as it was, there was an engine to be tinkered with, wasn't there? Not like some silly old carriage which could only move if you hitched a horse on to the front of it. And so the wordy battles went on, and on, and on.

Of all the old customs the one which seems to have aroused the most fury was the habit of making a curious noise while grooming a horse. The purpose of this 'zzzzzz' was to prevent dust and hair being inhaled, and also it soothed the horses. On the chauffeurs it had precisely the opposite effect. One chauffeur, with the sound buzzing in his ears like an angry wasp, noticed that a certain coachman had allowed the finger nails of one hand to grow abnormally long. Not being on speaking terms with the coachman he was unable to ask him why, and it was only when he saw the coachman run his fingers through a horse's mane like a comb that he realized the purpose. If the coachman had grown his canine teeth long and announced that he was a vampire, the chauffeur could not have regarded him with more horrified incredulity.

Another owner who vented his feelings in the correspondence columns of *The Autocar* was outraged by the behaviour of a friend's chauffeur. 'About seven o'clock in the evening a car was driven into my stableyard, and, on enquiring what the driver wanted, I was told, "I've come for young X." Young X had been spending the day with my young people but had driven off an hour before in a friend's pony cart as the car had not come, the said car arriving an hour late. I told him that my young friend had gone, and that he had been kept waiting, adding, "Are you Mr X's servant?" He stared at me blankly. "No," he said, "I'm his driver." Without further words he lit a very nasty cigarette, puffed the smoke almost in my face and off with him. I related the scene to my friend X, who told me that this fellow had absolutely declined either to touch his hat or to say "sir" on any occasion. I remarked on his rather grimy dress and was told he would not wear livery. A really charming person to have about the place at three pounds a week and all impertinences free.'

Why, one asks oneself, did not Mr X sack the man if he was as bad as all that? The answer must surely be that either Mr X and the querulous friend who rushed into print were exaggerating, or that the supply of chauffeurs was so limited that employers had to put up with what they could get. The truth probably lies somewhere in between. The supply of competent chauffeurs was, in the early years, undoubtedly strictly limited, and employers were resigned to the necessity of tolerating some shortcomings. But X's case, if true, shows such antagonism that it is astonishing that neither party brought it to a swift end.

As in any situation where demand exceeds supply, the chauffeur was in a powerful position. And if he were so minded he could exasperate his employer far beyond the point which would have ensured the dismissal of any more easily replaceable servant. Fortunately the great majority of chauffeurs do not seem to have been in a permanent state of sullen revolt. They had taken up chauffering out of a genuine interest in machinery and were intrigued by the possibilities of the motor car.

They learned all they could about it but did not trouble to learn what sort of behaviour was expected of them. All other servants had some kind of indoctrination when they first found employment, but there was nobody to teach the chauffeur. He had to work it out for himself, and sometimes he did not bother.

Curiously enough, this difficulty did not become apparent in the very early days of motoring. This was because chauffeur and employer shared a common interest and spent a lot of time in each other's company. 'A man may have a coachman in his service for twenty years and not become as intimately acquainted with his characteristics as he is with the motor-man who has been engaged a week. A common interest in "her" breeds a familiarity which is unknown in any other connection. Education has nothing to say in the matter, for very many motor-men would, in any other capacity, fall below the board school standard.' So wrote a correspondent to *The Court Journal*.

But as ownership of cars spread from the out-and-out enthusiast pioneer to the people who knew nothing of the technicalities and simply regarded the motor as a possible alternative to the carriage, this intimacy between chauffeur and employer was lost, and the complaints began. Employers were vociferous about lack of respect, cigarette-smoking, slovenly turn-out and a hundred minor irritations. Chauffeurs complained about their employers' ignorance which led them to make unreasonable demands, and to fail to make reasonable allowances. As one chauffeur put it, 'If the car goes well, the manufacturer gets the praise. If it goes badly, the chauffeur gets the blame.'

In the ten years between 1895 and 1905 the general attitude of employers towards chauffeurs went through two distinct phases. At first chauffeurs were companions, sharing a new enthusiasm. Then, as people other than enthusiasts became owners, chauffeurs were regarded in the light of visiting experts, and however much you disapproved of their behaviour you kept your opinions to yourself. You would no more correct your chauffeur than you would tell the visiting veterinary surgeon to take that cigarette out of his mouth, or the visiting plumber to smarten himself up. What really concerned the employer was that the man understood his mystery, and whether you liked him or not you had to treat him with respect, like the priest of some esoteric cult.

In both these phases the chauffeur was able to command high wages – often six pounds to a butler's five. But after about 1905 there was a sudden change in his fortunes.

It is impossible, particularly in times of inflation, to make accurate comparisons between values of money at different periods, but the chauffeur's wage of six pounds per week was well above the average earned at the factory work bench. Consequently many men were attracted from the factories. They were, on the whole, proficient engineers but wholly inexperienced as servants, and the fact that there were so many of them allowed employers to be more selective. For the first time supply was exceeding demand, and as required standards rose, so wages fell. From the heady six pounds the rate dropped steadily, and by about 1907 two pounds ten shillings was regarded as the going rate for the job.

Chauffeurs had been a race apart, their technical skills entitling them to be regarded with awe. Now they were looked upon quite differently. The novelty had worn off, and they were simply required to get on with the job, and to get on with it in a satisfactory manner. They could no longer expect to be treated as temperamental geniuses.

How quickly the chauffeur accepted this change in the attitude towards his role depended on his background. If he had come from a factory he was likely to resent the fact that the knowledge which he had acquired and the expertise which he had developed were all taken for granted. Furthermore, he felt restricted by being always on call. At the factory his time had been his own after he clocked off for the day and remained his own until he clocked on again next morning. Now he could expect no regular hours. At any time there might be an early train to catch or a party to take to the theatre and bring home afterwards. However considerate the employer might be, the chauffeur's time was not his own. Chauffeurs who had started as private servants – garden boys, grooms, footmen or whatever – accepted the restriction more readily. To them the discipline of a servant was already a way of life. While the man from the factory was apt to think that there was something humiliating about touching his hat to his employer and calling him 'sir', the man who had previously been employed as a servant took it as a matter of course.

'The old type of groom grew to be almost one of the family he served,' wrote a correspondent to *The Autocar*. 'He watched the children of the house grow up; the joys and sorrows and successes were shared by him, and he came to be more than a mere servant. I question whether this is so with the average chauffeur, or whether time will ever make it so.'

He may have been right about the 'average' chauffeur. He certainly was not right about the best of them. Men like Peter Robertson quickly became trusted and respected members of the household, deeply involved

with the doings of the family. They had already begun to show that in
the years to come the chauffeur would, in the happier establishments,
hold a uniquely individual position equivalent in authority and
responsibility to that of the old family butler. But in the early years of
the twentieth century chauffeurs were still too rare to have fitted
easily into any long-established tradition. They were too new a breed
to inspire confidence. They were not welcome in the servants' hall,
and they were often regarded with suspicion by their employers.

Except for grooms who had been retrained, the most acceptable
chauffeurs were ex-servicemen, and the Victoria Street offices of the
National Association for the Employment of Reserve and Discharged
Soldiers were kept busy with applications. An animated correspondence developed on the subject of which type of soldier made the best
chauffeur. 'The ideal chauffeur is an ex-Horse Artillery driver with
seven years' service and an exemplary character,' pronounced one
correspondent. Another countered with '. . . the cavalry make the best
chauffeurs; they are thoroughly disciplined and know their place, and,
having a natural love of sport, they are delighted to look after their
master's horses and dogs, and keep the guns in order, and on a long
journey they are the most charmingly breezy companions.' One
cannot help wondering whether, if the car broke down on one of those
long journeys, this enthusiast for the cavalry might not perhaps have
preferred the companionship of a man less charmingly breezy but
who had served his apprenticeship in the factory which produced the
car.

But wherever the chauffeur came from, his very coming heralded a
new era. And the exciting thing was that everybody realized that it
was a new era. One old pensioner has a clear memory of a red-letter
day when he was a little boy. His parents lived above a coach house in
Harley Mews, for his father was coachman to an eminent surgeon in
Harley Street. His brother was several years older and, after learning
by helping his father, he went off to be a groom in the service of the
surgeon's brother. He was not a good correspondent, and his family
did not hear from him for months at a time. Then, suddenly one day –
this never-to-be-forgotten day – there was a commotion at the end of
the mews and in swept the first car which had ever been seen there.
And, as if this were not enough excitement for the little boy, from this
glorious contraption, all glowing brass and shiny paint, stepped down
the godlike figure of his elder brother.

'All the old coachmen gathered round spellbound. The doctors from Harley Street and Weymouth Street came to the windows of their consulting rooms to gaze at this new and wonderful invention. We in the family were very proud.'

The child, dancing with excitement, glanced up at his father and was astonished to see that there were tears in the old coachman's eyes. He shook his head slowly and turned to his wife. 'Louisa,' he said sadly, 'this is the beginning of the end for horse-drawn carriages.'

5

'Gladly Wolde He Lerne'

Geoffrey Chaucer

While a mechanic working in a motor car factory found plenty of opportunities of learning how to drive, it was much more difficult for anybody else. A soldier demobilized after the Boer War, or a groom tired of horses might decide that he would like to become a chauffeur, but his great problem was to know where to start. Some sought out men who could drive already and begged them to explain the basic methods of controlling a car; others just picked it up as they went along. One young man who was methodical about it was William Hollingsworth, who worked his way up from pageboy in the household of Mrs Walter Evans. By 1903 he was a fully fledged footman and used to accompany the coachman whenever the carriage went out.

William was fascinated by cars and longed to learn to drive one. A couple of years later his opportunity came when a small legacy from an aunt enabled him to go to London where there was a primitive sort of driving school in Notting Hill Gate. On completing the course he obtained, in 1906, a job as fourth chauffeur to Sir Clive Morrison Bell at Otterburn Hall in Northumberland. In his lowly position he was only permitted to drive the estate hack, an Oldsmobile with a wagonette body which jolted and jarred its way round the moorland tracks. But living conditions were good, the pay was good, and he felt that he had made a start on his career as a chauffeur. He moved on to a position where he was the sole chauffeur in a rather more modest establishment, and he would probably have remained there if Mrs Evans had not decided that the time had come for her to have a car, and asked William to return to her employment. She consulted him about the type of car to buy and, on his advice, bought a Daimler landaulette. Except for a break for war service in the Royal Flying Corps he remained with Mrs Evans until her death in 1929.

A rather less well organized start to a chauffeur's career was made by Rupert Harwood, the son of the Marlow blacksmith. After serving in the Royal Engineers he returned to Marlow where he was offered a job by a Doctor Nicholson. Neither of them could drive, but this does not seem to have deterred the doctor from buying a car to take him on his rounds. With the black bag in the back, and Rupert at the wheel, the doctor would seat himself in the front and read out commands from the instruction book.

Both of them survived this hazardous initiation and Rupert, like William, remained a chauffeur for the rest of his working life. The open air life which they led in the early days, perched high up with no protection from the weather, must have suited these two pioneer chauffeurs, for each of them lived until he was over ninety.

In the first decade of the twentieth century many of the large estates were still as self-sufficient as they had been a couple of hundred years before. They grew their own food, they made their own amusements and entertainment, and, above all, they created their own facilities for learning new skills. Such a one was Oulton Park, where Sir Philip Grey Egerton decided that the time had come to take notice of these new motors. It would not have occurred to him to engage a man from outside. He had seven perfectly good grooms and one of them was eager to learn to drive.

Accordingly they laid out a driving course in the park, using beer bottles as markers. Sir Philip, his Agent, the Agent's assistant and the groom designated to be a chauffeur spent many happy hours manoeuvring round this strange precursor of the Oulton Park racing circuit which, over two generations later, would test the abilities of the country's finest drivers.

Oulton Park had wide open spaces where nothing was likely to come to harm except the beer bottles (and they were, presumably, empty), but driving practice in a confined space could be expensive. One owner who encouraged his grooms to learn to drive found that his own and visiting cars so often bashed into the wall of the stableyard that he had a high pavement built out from it. After that the cars stopped with a jolt when their tyres hit the pavement and any damage was limited to the tyres themselves.

The school which William Hollingsworth attended, the Motor Academy, had been founded primarily for owners, but many would-be chauffeurs also made use of it and it soon branched out, even to the extent of having dual control vehicles specially made by a Coventry firm. In the first ten years of the century driving schools mushroomed up, usually issuing their pupils with impressive diplomas. One such proclaimed that the student had 'undergone a thorough course of instruction at the schools of THE MOTOR DRIVERS UNION, in Motor Car Mechanism, the Driving of Motor Cars in and out of traffic, the Rules of the Road, and the Various Regulations respecting Motor Cars with which a Chauffeur should be familiar: in all of which branches he has satisfactorily demonstrated his proficiency.'

What must have been one of the earliest schools was advertising in the *Strand* magazine in 1903. But it was not until five years later that a very small acorn was planted by Stanley Roberts, the son of a doctor. He was mad about cars, and wanted to earn his living in some way connected with them, but he did not know quite what. One day a coachman, seeing him get out of the doctor's car, asked how he had learned to drive. The conversation soon turned to the coachman's own ambitions to become a chauffeur, and to Stanley Roberts's delighted surprise he found himself being asked to instruct the coachman, who was willing to pay for the lessons. The idea of earning his living by the thoroughly enjoyable means of driving about all day enchanted Roberts. He soon talked his father into allowing him the use of a shed behind the stables in Peckham, and in 1910 he set up a regular business employing a qualified mechanic, a slightly less qualified mechanic (ten shillings a week less), and two boys desperately keen to learn all about motors. Soon Roberts engaged a couple of extra instructors, one of whom was Archie Frazer-Nash whose chain-driven sports cars were the idols of every enthusiast twenty years later.

In 1912 Stanley Roberts changed the name of his company from S. Roberts & Co to the more grandiose one of 'The British School of Motoring', a name which seventy years later is entirely appropriate to that organization which has branches all over the country.

But in Edwardian times only a handful of chauffeurs received professional instruction, and it was not until 1935 that the system of provisional licences and driving tests was introduced. Ex-coachmen had an advantage in that they were experienced in judging speed and distance and in taking their place amongst other traffic. But guiding a pair of horses with a gentle pressure on the reins was quite a different matter from the heaving and tugging required to persuade a motor to change direction. All early drivers experienced difficulty with changing gear, but for the chauffeur the problems were increased by stiff and clumsy boots and leggings. These were necessary for keeping wet weather at bay, but they were not conducive to delicate footwork.

Chauffeurs to enthusiastic owners soon began to take a pride in their driving but the increasing number of people who regarded a motor as a carriage which ran on petrol instead of hay and neither knew, nor wished to know, anything more about it were quite unconcerned with the standard of driving. Indeed, beyond reproving the chauffeur for 'scorching' if they bumped about too much, most passengers left it all to the man at the wheel.

Chauffeurs who were accustomed to working for employers who did not themselves drive never received encouragement to improve their technique. One ex-coachman never learned to reverse at all, but he knew the country lanes near his base so well that he was able to plan a circuitous route without ever being faced with the necessity of turning round. He wisely never ventured beyond the immediate neighbourhood of a singularly traffic-free part of Ireland. But another Irishman, more adventurous although no more skilled, embarked on a highly unsuitable career as a chauffeur in London. Inevitably he had many a brush with the Law but he always managed to get away with his misdoings by pretending that he was Welsh and could speak no other tongue. He reckoned, correctly, that the chances of an encounter with a Welsh policeman were slight enough to disregard.

One ex-coachman who had been driving badly for thirty years finally got a job with a man whose previous chauffeur had driven smoothly and well. He did not take kindly to the sudden lurches, the abrupt stops and the way the car would take off like a terrified kangaroo every time the new chauffeur let in the clutch. But the employer was a considerate man and did not like to criticize too harshly, so he simply made a gentle suggestion. The chauffeur, puzzled that anybody should find fault with a performance with which he himself had been perfectly satisfied, but nevertheless anxious to oblige, sought enlightenment from a fellow chauffeur. 'My gov'nor says I ought to drive with more finesse,' he announced. 'What the f——g 'ell's finesse?'

Although undoubtedly lacking in polish, his driving had at least been done on cars, whereas a farm labourer who applied for a job in

1912 had hitherto driven only steam traction engines. He persuaded a farming friend to fake a reference for him. By the simple means of saying 'yes' when the true answer would have been 'no', he obtained the position of chauffeur to a man who had not previously owned a car but was just expecting delivery of a brand new Mettalurgique. Car and chauffeur arrived simultaneously, from different directions. The car was elegant, resplendent in silver-grey paint and glittering brass. The chauffeur's appearance is not recorded.

The new owner, beside himself with pride and excitement, organized a theatre party in celebration, and off they went to the Hippodrome in Southend. It was only a short distance and they were in far too great a state of euphoria to notice anything as mundane as the quality of the chauffeur's driving. Besides, they were not used to cars.

On arrival at the theatre they dismounted and the owner, now bulging with importance, issued precise orders to the chauffeur about collecting them after the play.

When, in due course, the party emerged from the theatre there was no car, no chauffeur. It could not have been more of an anticlimax if, on their arrival, the curtain had gone up to reveal an empty stage. Where *could* the chauffeur have got to? What can he have been doing?

They went on asking each these questions in increasingly querulous tones for the next half-hour. Finally somebody suggested to the owner, timidly, that perhaps it might be as well to try to find a horse-drawn cab to take them home. Looking like Napoleon when he first heard the suggestion that the time had come to leave Moscow, he reluctantly sanctioned this plan. Those who thought that this moment marked the nadir of the evening were in for a shock. And, at that moment, round the corner it came. A sad travesty of the once-proud Metallurgique limped into view, one wing dolefully flapping, one headlamp dulled and dented, pointing skywards as if in supplication. The answer to the question 'What can the chauffeur have been doing?' was abundantly obvious. He had been having an accident.

The car seemed to be entirely covered in mud, but at least it had shown itself to be still drivable. The chastened party clambered in.

But if they thought that the night held no more horrors they were mistaken. The interior of the car was filthy. Not just muddy and damp but, well, filthy. It was, as one member of the party put it, like a pigsty. In fact this was a shrewd assessment because the most recent inhabitant had been a pig. The chauffeur, triumphant at having conned his way into the job, had taken the opportunity of the family being at the theatre to take the car to show to his accomplice. Near his friend's cottage he met him, driving a pig along the lane. In expansive mood he offered a lift to both friend and pig. It seemed a good idea at the time.

On the way back he hit a wall.

It was small consolation to the enraged employer to refuse a reference to the chauffeur whom he dismissed next day. The pig-owner would no doubt oblige with another fake.

Throughout the whole story of chauffeuring the theme of references runs like a thread. It was – and is – a most unsatisfactory system because an employer seldom writes what he means. The law of libel hangs over the entire scene and its threat distorts the meaning of the simplest phrase. An employer who wanted to say that his chauffeur was drunken, dirty, and dishonest did not dare to do so. Either he refused a reference altogether – and there was always the danger that he might find himself having to justify that action in court – or he told a flat lie. If, on the other hand the chauffeur had served him well and he wanted to say so, his praise would often be discounted by the reader. It was common practice to give an over-fulsome reference to a servant who had not given specific reason to warrant dismissal. It might be that the chauffeur did not get on with the cook, or got on too well with the housemaid, or simply that the employer could not bear to travel a mile more behind a man whose ears stuck out like that. In cases such as these he would salve his conscience by writing an enthusiastic reference scattered with superlatives.

Even the most upright employer would indulge in a little gentle deception and, for a prospective employer, the art lay in interpreting the code and reading between the lines of euphemism. What was not said was more important than what was said. For instance, 'He is leaving my service because I have given up motoring' might be perfectly true, but the reader's view of the applicant might be different if the reference continued, '. . . I am giving up motoring because my car is a total write-off after the chauffeur drove it through the garage wall while drunk.'

Many an employer engaged in writing a reference which he knew would be read by its subject must have envied the freedom of the cavalry colonel who could write, secure in the knowledge that the subaltern concerned would never be shown the confidential report, 'Personally I would not breed from this officer.'

6

Start up, James

As long as the chauffeur did not actually hit anything, it did not greatly matter whether he was a good driver or not. There was so little traffic in the early years of the century that he had to be a very bad driver indeed before his passengers noticed it.

On the other hand it was absolutely essential the he should be a good enough mechanic to maintain the car himself, and to repair it if it broke down. Modern cars are infinitely more complicated than ancient ones but they require very little attention. Early cars may have been delightfully simple but they needed to be constantly attended to. Chauffeurs were eternally oiling and greasing them, topping them up with water for the acetylene gas headlights, paraffin for the side- and tail-lights, and if they did not lubricate the cone clutch every couple of days it would start screeching. Before the days of chokes they would stuff a rag dipped in petrol into the carburettor intake to aid starting from cold.

It was not until 1912 that Cadillac pioneered self-starters, and previously the only way of starting a stationary car was by swinging the handle. This in itself required a certain expertise as well as brute force because when the engine fired the handle was apt to swing round and break the wrist of the man holding it. One rich and prudent owner, aware of this danger, always had a spare chauffeur sitting beside the driver in case of emergency. Even though, in those lavish days, an extra servant here or there did not matter much, most owners confined themselves to one driver, relying on his instinct of self-preservation to see them safely home.

The very first thing that any would-be chauffeur was taught was the correct method of wielding the starting-handle. It should be cupped in the palm of the hand with the fingers straight up so that immediately the engine fired the handle would leave the hand. As long as the fingers were not clenched the man's arm would not be wrenched, and if he withdrew it smartly enough he would be out of the way before the handle came swishing viciously round again. The trick was to ease the handle slowly on the down stroke and pull it up sharply.

Once the engine was started the chauffeur not unnaturally liked to keep it running, and this is the reason why so many photographs taken outside front doors show chauffeurs standing clearcut like statues fashioned with a very sharp chisel while behind them is a blurred mass of motor quivering like water heaving itself to the boil.

An alternative, much favoured by chauffeurs, to all this laborious and perilous manual toil was to let the car coast downhill with a gear (usually second or third) engaged and the clutch out. When he judged the speed to be high enough the chauffeur would let in the clutch and, at least in theory, the engine would fire. Failure to start by this method was ominous and presaged much fruitless swinging of the handle when the level ground had been reached and the car come to rest. Such store was set by having a convenient hill very near the garage that one chauffeur announced to his employer, who was thinking of moving, that if the new house was on level ground he would hand in his notice. Which of them won this battle of wills and hills is not recorded.

After the haunting anxiety as to whether the engine would burst into joyous sound or remain sullenly silent came the worry over tyres. Reasonably reliable on bicycles, tyres before the First World War had not been developed sufficiently to cope with the weight and speed of cars. They frequently burst, and a journey without a puncture was considered remarkably good fortune. An ample supply of spares had to be carried, and if you ran out of inner tubes you stuffed the tyre with hay or grass as a last resort. (One ex-chauffeur remembered this trick when he was serving as a scout car driver in the Western Desert during the Second World War. When he had come to the end of his inner tubes he tried packing the tyres with sand. It did not work.)

Manipulating heavy levers to prise the stiff rubber away from the rims was one of the chauffeur's least pleasant tasks, particularly as it had to be carried out wherever the puncture occurred – for, in the first years of the century, there were only spare tyres and no spare wheels.

Life became easier with the invention of detachable rims and also the 'Stepney', a rim and tyre which could be bolted on beside the flat tyre. Right up to the Second World War it was normal for cars which were big enough to have room for them to be supplied with two spare wheels, although by that time tyres and tubes were much more reliable and road surfaces smoother. The sharp flints, and the nails from horses' hooves no longer lay in wait to penetrate the first tyre which bowled over them.

Another hazard which threatened the early chauffeurs was the prospect of running out of petrol. A pony trap or wagonette would bring a quantity of tins from the nearest – though usually fairly distant – garage, and they were stored with little regard to fire risk in the private motor house. These stout tins contained two gallons each, and it was usual to carry a full one on the running board. Many a chauffeur remembers the sinking feeling he experienced when, on lifting the can, he found it ominously light – either because the cap had become loose and the petrol had evaporated or because, after last time, he had forgotten to replace it with a full one. Cars were expected to break down, it was part of the natural order of things, and only the most unreasonable employer took exception when they did. But running out of petrol was quite another matter. It was obvious and indisputable proof of the chauffeur's incompetence. He would consider his employer to be kind, weak or idiotic if he were not instantly dismissed.

One thing which had to be tolerated by chauffeurs and employer alike was the facetious or mocking comments made by people walking or riding by a car stranded by the roadside. Peter Robertson was once executing some repair with the assistance of his employer's son. They were both spreadeagled in the mud, heaving at recalcitrant spanners, when a clergyman approached on a bicycle. He bestowed a sunny smile on them and remarked, 'Just like a comic postcard.'

The two young men wriggled out from under and, speaking no word, they snatched up handfuls of mud and flung them at the receding clerical back.

Had he but known it, the clergyman was fortunate that it had been raining, for if it had been fine the mud would have turned to dust which cannot be thrown. His assailants would then no doubt have had recourse to one of the piles of stones which were a common roadside feature before the days of tarring.

Sometimes, of course, passers-by were anxious to help, though their assistance was usually of limited value. An extreme case was that of a veterinary surgeon returning from a hard day at the market where he had met a large number of clients. He was snoozing happily in his pony trap when some noise aroused him, and he saw a car by the side of the road. Its bonnet was open and the chauffeur was bending over the engine. The vet was half asleep and more than half drunk, but in benevolent mood. He must, he felt, render assistance. Clambering carefully down he lifted out the black bag which always accompanied him, and opened it. He did not know what to do but the urge to help was strong. He racked his bemused brains, frowning in concentration.

Suddenly his brow cleared. A familiar sight had cut through the alcoholic haze. It was a large brown bottle, conspicuously labelled 'Cow Cough Mixture'.

The vet fingered it lovingly. 'Shplendid shtuff!' he announced. 'Shplendid shtuff! Never fails. Never fails. Never, never, never fails.'

Uncorking the bottle he poured a solemn libation over the engine.

As it happened the chauffeur had cleared the obstruction in the fuel pipe by this time and was at that moment turning the starting handle. As the cough mixture trickled over the engine the ignition fired and the car pulsated into life.

The vet uttered a triumphant cry and, pocketing a small fee for his cough mixture, he climbed happily back into his trap and swept off.

7

From Coach-House to Motor House

With little traffic and with cars which were only at one remove from the experimental stage, it was natural that employers should place more emphasis on mechanical than driving ability. Typical of many is one eighteen-year-old lad who started work in a garage and took a prospective purchaser for a trial run. They had not got very far when the car broke down. The customer was a doctor and the thought of being stranded on his way to an urgent case made him immediately rule out his idea of buying a car. He began to look about for some safe, horse-drawn vehicle to give him a lift home.

However, the boy assured him that he knew exactly what had caused the breakdown, and it that it would take less than fifteen minutes to put right. The doctor watched fascinated by the deft skill with which the young mechanic handled what the doctor mentally classified as the mechanical patient. With a chauffeur who understood its ailments as thoroughly as that, a motor car could reasonably be considered reliable transport. Accordingly the doctor bought the car and engaged the boy as chauffeur. Everybody was highly delighted – except the garage owner, who was loath to lose a likely lad. But he was even more loath to lose a sale, so he let him go. Thus began the career of a chauffeur who was to remain with the same family for the whole of his working life – a full fifty years, except for war service from 1914 to 1918, during which time his job was kept open for him.

Especially in the country the car was usually kept at some distance from a service station, and so for maintenance as well as emergency repairs the chauffeur had to rely on his own resources. The employers understood that the money laid out for the purchase of the car was only a part of the expenditure involved, and many of them set up elaborate workshops. This was accepted as a necessary concomitant of car ownership, and on large estates it became part of the general policy of improvement and replacement. The motor needed its workshop just as the herd needed its dairy.

In the same way that the motor was gradually taking over the functions of the carriage, so part of the spacious accommodation designed for the horse and horse-drawn vehicles was adapted for the car. One of the coach-houses would become the motor house, a stable would become a workshop, another might be a store for tyres and spare parts. The chauffeurs being the men who were to operate the system, they were closely consulted at every step, and this led to an increased importance in their position. From being simply one servant among many the chauffeur became, like the butler or head gardener, the head of his own department of the estate, even if he was the only man in it.

A particularly lavish scheme – though no doubt considered quite ordinary in those spacious Edwardian days – is here described in detail:

. . . the sick box was made into a mechanic's workshop, with bench, lathe, drills, etc, and a store for oil drums and spare acetylene cylinders for headlights. A battery charging plant was fitted into the coach-house. An inspection pit was dug into the floor so that a car could be driven over the pit and a man could work underneath standing upright to check brakes, springs, etc, using a hand electric lamp on a long cable, its bulb protected by a wire cage. The floor of the coach-house was concrete, but large tin trays containing an inch of sand were put under the engine and back axle to collect oil which frequently leaked out under the car. These trays were also carried out to the drive when visiting cars called, so that no drips of oil should stain the gravel. Petrol was delivered once a month by horse and dray, in two-gallon tins painted red. These were stored in a steel cabinet with two ventilators at the top, and locked with a large padlock. It was sited at the bottom of the stableyard away from all buildings because of the fire risk.

An inspection pit was almost essential because twenty or thirty grease nipples, which could only be reached from beneath the car, needed attention very often indeed, some of them every time the car went out. Peter Robertson and his employer enthusiastically super-vised the ripping up of the flagstones in the building which had once held Nell Gwynn's coaches so that a pit could be dug.

No garage was without its bench, few without a lathe. The earliest lathes were worked by treadle but most were later motorized.

All this lavish equipment was thoroughly well used. Keeping those temperamental cars in running order was a formidable task and, besides the everyday maintenance, it was customary for the chauffeur to carry out a complete overhaul every year, a routine matter which everybody took for granted, like spring-cleaning the house. It was scheduled to coincide with one of the family's annual absences from home, if they were in the habit of remaining in one place for a sufficiently long period.

In the days when cars were almost entirely hand-built there was an infinite variety of options available, some owners having two bodies made, an open one for summer and a closed one for winter. When the time came to change over, an elaborate system of pulleys and winches would lift one body of the chassis, with all available local manpower shoving and heaving until it could be lowered on to a stage of planks or, more often, four barrels. Chauffeurs preferred barrels because it was easier to get under the body to strip, rub down, and repaint the frame.

Even when there was not an alternative to replace it the body was usually lifted off during the annual overhaul. In some cases this operation would take place at the coachbuilder's so that the coachwork could be professionally painted and varnished, and any necessary repairs and replacements made to the upholstery and carpets. If it was an open car, as many were, with a leather hood, that too would be treated. But if the body never left the owner's garage it would nevertheless receive attention, and it was likely that repainting would form part of the annual overhaul. Chauffeurs became expert at do-it-yourself decorating, and in most cases it was only necessary to call in professional assistance for such things as painting the family crest on the panels or freshening up the coachlines along the bonnet. After the brushwork was finished to his satisfaction, absolutely smooth with no lumps or furrows, the chauffeur would carefully apply coats of clear varnish, which he hoped would ward off the effects of dust and slush until the varnish cracked and assumed a yellowish tinge, whereupon the next refurbishment was due.

The overhaul of the chassis was extraordinarily comprehensive. Gearboxes would be stripped down and worn parts replaced, springs would be dismantled leaf by leaf, scrupulously cleaned and then reassembled with a packing of graphite grease. In fact every moving part would be closely examined and anything which showed the slightest sign of wear would be renewed. With the low-octane petrol and the low compression ratios of engines, they frequently needed to be decarbonized. This entailed 'grinding in' the valves and polishing them with a mild abrasive such as knife powder mixed with oil. A good chauffeur would go on polishing until he achieved a clear mirror-like finish with not the least blemish of the carbon to settle on. All washers and bearings, rods and levers, pipes and hoses, were subjected to the same meticulous scrutiny.

When the chauffeur had dismantled everything he could think of, he put it together again and hoped it would work. It usually did. But after an overhaul the car had almost to be 'run in' all over again. Until the new parts had settled down, mysterious rattles and squeaks would make their appearance, and it usually meant that the chauffeur had to make several trips before their cause was located and eradicated. Often he did this testing seated on a box bolted to the chassis frame. It made tracing the faults and remedying them far easier if he could work on the bare chassis, and there was so little protection for the chauffeur on early cars that it did not make much difference when that little was removed.

It is remarkable how quickly chauffeurs, that 'new breed' of servants, adapted themselves to established customs. The resentment of the pioneers against the standards of domestic service very soon gave way not merely to an acceptance of those standards but to pride in them. The first of the 'new breed' may have scoffed at the coachmen, but as one chauffeur who started his career in Edwardian times put it, 'I met many ex-coachman chauffeurs who always seemed to treat their motors with the same gentle regard that they had had for their horses. They took great pride in cleaning their vehicles.'

Cleaning things to a very high standard of polish formed a big part of the life of any Edwardian servant. In a sizeable establishment there would be a boy to clean the knives (no stainless steel blades then) and those boots and shoes which were not in the valet's special care; kitchen-maids would black-lead stoves and rub them until they took on the glassy sheen of jet; housemaids would burnish fenders and pokers, footmen would spend hours polishing all the silver except those few items which were so particularly precious that only the butler himself laid his dignified hands upon them. Inside these huge houses everything shone and glowed, and under the watchful eye of the housekeeper the floors and furniture gleamed like steady beacons. The faint aroma of beeswax hung like a benediction over these stately rooms.

Outside, teams of gardeners rolled and raked the gravel, clipped the hedges as carefully as any barber expecting a lavish tip, and guided the donkeys or ponies pulling mowers across the acres of lawns. Lest the hooves should indent the billiards-table smoothness of the grass they were encased in leather bootees, and any trace of the animal's passage was immediately removed with brush and shovel.

A chauffeur would have had to be very bloody-minded to stand out against this general acceptance of perfection as the only possible standard, and the majority of chauffeurs were not bloody-minded at all. They gloried in keeping their cars spotless. This was a difficult task because of the condition of the roads. A car needed to be driven only a couple of miles for everything to assume a thick coating of dust which turned to mud as soon as it rained. At the beginning of the twentieth century roads were probably in a worse state than they had been at the beginning of the nineteenth. It was not until Regency times that much attention had been paid to them and then, following the Industrial Revolution, great emphasis was placed on fast communication. Civil engineers like John Macadam took the matter in hand and produced a network of well-surfaced roads, the like of which Britain had not seen since Roman times. With sound drainage and foundations the roads were able to stand up to the greatly increased traffic, and stage coaches would bowl along at a spanking rate, while the Regency bucks wagered enormous sums on the number of minutes their curricles could clip off the four hours of the journey from London to Brighton.

But the road revival was short-lived. Very soon the railways took on from where the stage-coaches left off, and the roads were deserted by all except local traffic. When pot-holes developed they were not filled in, and grass grew along the middle of the roads which had been deliberately left rough and gravelly to give a good grip to horses' hooves. As late as 1895 H. G. Wells was able to base his light novel *The Wheels of Chance* on the theme of tracking a couple of bicycles down the dusty lanes which formed the main roads of Sussex. The hero, Mr Hoopdriver, was intent upon saving the heroine from a fate worse than falling off and was greatly dismayed when he lost the 'spoor' on the cobbles of Chichester. Disconsolate he cast about, finally he tried 'the road towards Bognor, kicking up the dust with his shoes and fretting with disappointed pugnacity. A thwarted, crestfallen Hoopdriver it was, as you may well imagine. And then suddenly there jumped upon his attention – a broad line ribbed like a shilling, and close beside it one chequered, that ever and again split into two.'

Throughout the twentieth century roads have improved steadily but, particularly in the early years, never fast enough, and the dust which was kicked up caused chauffeurs to fret just as much as Mr Hoopdriver did. In fact probably more, because their machines were bigger than his and took longer to clean.

Chauffeurs driving in London did not, of course, have the dust problem, but before the invention of smokeless fuels the 'pea-soup' fogs covered everything with a greasy black deposit.

One of the fundamental rules of coachmen was that the carriage should be cleaned directly it came in, however late that might be, and chauffeurs came to accept this rule without question, although some of them were not above modifying it to suit special circumstances. After a very late night a chauffeur might clean only the side of the car which his employer could see when he stepped into it next morning. But this was acknowledged to be a risky thing to do and was frowned upon by the more responsible ones.

To clean a car properly meant taking off each wheel in turn, washing it with sponge and spoke-brush and not replacing it until the underside of the mudwing had been similarly attended to. The front axle and brake drums were coated with black lead, like the kitchen range, and then vigorously brushed until they shone. The washing of the coachwork was like some great cult ceremony. First the chauffeur would don overhauls and fishing waders. Then would begin the assembling of the ritual equipment – the buckets, the sponges, the soft chamois leathers. The leathers, particularly, were jealously guarded and the chauffeur regarded them as his personal property exclusively for his own use.

The actual means employed varied. Some chauffeurs liked to use warm water, others cold. Some worked soft soap up to a lather, others put a few drops of paraffin in the water. But whichever way the chauffeur chose he was totally convinced of two things. Firstly that his car was cleaner than anybody else's and secondly that his way of doing things was superior. When discussing the matter with other chauffeurs he was torn between boasting of his own cleverness, and keeping his precious secrets to himself. Only if he could be quite sure that his ideas were not going to be appropriated might he mention casually to a London-based colleague that the important thing was to use only rainwater and that he happened to be fortunate that his employer's country house was well endowed with water butts.

Some of the little devices used by chauffeurs for making life easier were not secrets at all, and were widely employed. For instance, before there was any method of heating windscreens, rubbing them with half a potato might save the chauffeur having to drive with the screen open in freezing fog. Better for cleaning glass than all the sponges and leathers was a newspaper, moistened but not too wet otherwise it disintegrated and left bits of fluff on the windows. *The Times* was considered best for the purpose because of the thickness of its pages. For lighting fires housemaids found the popular press more satisfactorily volatile.

Chauffeurs were not above consulting housemaids when it came to the business of keeping all that brass bright. Pipes all over the engine, lights and brackets and handles all needed constant attention if they were not to become dulled. In really bad weather the massive headlights might be taken off their brackets and left at home, if the chauffeur could be absolutely certain of finishing the journey in daylight; otherwise they might be discreetly covered. In any weather it was a common sight in Edwardian London for a chauffeur to be dusting his car while waiting outside a shop.

As tyres grew more reliable it became customary to paint the spares with shiny black paint and, later, the walls of the tyres on the road wheels might be painted white – a treatment which had to be repeated after every journey.

In the country cars might get dirtier, but cleaning them was easier than in the cramped conditions of a London mews. Not only were there convenient rainwater butts, plenty of room in the garage workshop for the buckets, brushes and dusters, while the sponges and leathers dried in the open air, but also there was invariably a 'wash'. This was of cobbles or concrete sloping to a drain in the middle. Usually it was sited so that it had the protection of a wall on one or, better still, two sides. It was roofed in, sometimes with glass, and it always had some form of artificial lighting. No self-respecting chauffeur would dream of taking a job where facilities for washing the car after dark were not provided. However long a journey, however many hours he had been working, however early he had to get up next day, no matter how late it was the chauffeur was supposed to clean the car directly he returned to the garage.

A considerable encouragement was the admiration of people who saw the car, gleaming in its glory. Each week a special time would be scheduled for the inspection, usually between Church and luncheon on

Sunday mornings. This inspection included the horses, the green-houses, perhaps the dairy and the pigsties, but always the car or cars, wheeled out of their garages and standing with their bonnets open to disclose the dazzle of brass and copper.

The Sunday morning inspection was a great feature of country house entertaining. It so neatly solved the problem of what to do with the huge house party on the one morning of the week when there could be no shooting or hunting, a problem which haunted the minds of hostesses who had been brought up to accept that if a hostess did not lay herself out to amuse her guests the guests were entitled to lay her out to amuse themselves. For the cloud which hung above those halcyon days before the First World War was the threat of boredom. Even if you called it *ennui*, boredom was still boredom, and the leisured classes devoted much ingenuity to warding it off. Reading the autobiographies of the period one often gets the impression that the higher echelons of the nobility and the financial world were constantly mobilized to keep Edward VII from falling victim to this dreaded malaise.

The advent of the car gave a welcome new interest to the routine of the Sunday inspection and not even the most languid members of that pampered generation could fail to be impressed by the magnificent appearance of those gleaming pipes, even though they may have had scant idea of what they were all for.

One hostess who took a particular pride, shared by her chauffeur, in the appearance of her limousine suffered almost as much as he did when he broke his leg and was laid up in hospital. She engaged a temporary one, but it was not the same thing at all. The brass lost its glitter, so did the silver vase attached to the partition. The violets in it withered and died, the sheepskin mat was never taken out and shaken. The new man did his best, but his best was pretty bad.

What made it all worse was that the lady was about to pay a visit to Cannes, a trip she made every year and, for the last two, by car. With her own trusted chauffeur at the wheel the leisurely journeys through France had been most enjoyable but she had grave doubts as to how she would fare with this new man. Her friends urged her to change her plans and go by train, but she would have none of it. Her whole Victorian upbringing had taught her to be indomitable, and to change her plans would be 'giving in', an unthinkable weakness. No, certainly not. She would go by car if it killed her.

It very nearly did. On the return journey the car skidded and ended up on its side in a ditch. But before that the chauffeur had justified her worst misgivings. He never seemed able to remember which side of the road he was supposed to be on. He left her dressing-case behind in Cannes, and they had to go back forty miles to retrieve it. Once he ran out of petrol, left the car unattended while he went to a café, and came back to find that the spare tyres had been stolen. On another occasion he neglected to tighten the straps on the luggage grid, and his employer's suitcase fell off, burst open, and strewed her underwear over Route Nationale 1.

She endured it all, erect and dignified on the back seat, her face impassive. At long last the journey was nearing its end and they had, in spite of everything, won through to within twenty miles of Dieppe – when the disaster struck. A sudden shower had made the road treacherous, a condition which the chauffeur had not observed. Anxious to get back to a country where he could understand what people said, he hastened on and swung too quickly round a corner. The topheavy car began to slide, and he had no idea how to control the skid. He sat petrified as the limousine slewed across the road and thumped into the high verge. For an instant it hung teetering and then thudded on to its side with a shrieking of tortured metal.

The lady in the back seat was miraculously unscathed as jagged lumps of plate glass flew about her head. Without losing an iota of dignity she clambered up through the door above her head and slid down on to the grass on which the wreck rested. Her face was ashen, but it was not with fright or shock. She was in a cold, deadly fury. Wholly ignoring the yammering of the unnerved chauffeur, she set off purposefully to get help. Then, after a few yards, she paused and turned round to survey the damage as the car lay there exposing its underbelly like an animal acknowledging defeat. For a moment she stood motionless, taking it all in and etching the scene on her memory for all time.

At last she directed her gaze at the chauffeur and addressed him for the first time since the accident. There was ice in her voice as she said, 'The underneath of that car is filthy.'

8

Keeping Royal Wheels Turning

In the course of her long reign Queen Victoria saw the expansion of railways from their tentative beginnings to an elaborate system criss-crossing the country. She came completely to terms with travel by train, provided that they did not go too *fast*, but by the time cars came on the scene she was too old and too tired to take any interest. It was left to the next generation to develop this exciting new way of getting about, and her son the Prince of Wales (soon to become King Edward VII) was, right from the start, keen on motoring and, after the second Lord Montagu had taken him for one of his first drives, he soon made up his mind to have a motor of his own. With due ceremony an order was placed for a 6-horsepower, 2-cylinder Daimler, and a body was constructed by Hooper, the famous St James's Street coachbuilders. The King was already in his sixtieth year when it was delivered in 1900, and although he had a few lessons on private roads he never really became a driver. From the very first he employed a chauffeur, and who better than the man who delivered the car, Sidney Henry Letzer? Thus the Daimler Company sold a car but lost a mechanic.

Proficient though he was as a driver, Letzer was unfamiliar with the roads round Windsor, and the first time he took the King out they were preceded by a groom on horseback who acted as guide. At Sandringham the function of outrider was performed by that dashing cavalryman, the Keeper of the Privy Purse, General Sir Dighton Probyn VC. But the chauffeur had six times as much power at his disposal as the rider, and the little car chugged steadily away from its escort.

The King was fascinated by his new toy, and was quick to see the potential of this new form of transport. He ordered more Daimlers, and by the time of his coronation, in June 1902, he had four of them, and took a great interest in them all. Queen Alexandra, too, liked motoring, but she was not as keen on speed as the King. When the car was drawn up in front of the door, Letzer, sitting motionless and staring straight ahead of him like a Guardsman on parade, could not see who got into the tonneau behind him. Occasionally the Queen's voice could be heard saying, 'I'm here today, Letzer,' so that he knew that he must maintain a sedate pace, with no scorching. That he was tactful enough to please the Queen as well as the King is evidenced by her gift to him of a book rivetingly entitled *The Automobile. A Practical Treatise of Modern Motor Cars, steam, petrol, electric, and petrol-electric.* It was inscribed 'For Letzer from Queen Alexandra, Xmas 1903', and is still in the possession of the chauffeur's daughter.

HRH The Duke of Kent, when opening the National Motor Museum at Beaulieu, in 1972, quoted from a letter which Queen Alexandra had written to her son in an early burst of enthusiasm for motoring: 'I enjoyed being driven about at 50 miles an hour . . . and I poked the driver violently in the back at every corner to make him go gently!

'Could it be,' the Duke mused, 'that my great-grandmother was the original backseat driver?'

The following year the cars were considered reliable enough to replace carriages as royal transport on all but the most formal occasions, and those two pillars of the Household establishment, The Keeper of the Privy Purse and the Crown Equerry, turned their attention to regulating the employment of the chauffeurs. Quarters were organized for them in the royal mews to save the 'large lodging allowance' which they were previously paid, and when they were at Sandringham, Windsor or Balmoral they had their own accommodation under the charge of a cook. Major General Sir Henry Ewart, the Crown Equerry, was conscious of social distinctions and suggested that Day, the washer, might remain in a 'cubicle, and not be located with the chauffeurs'.

Having started to make suggestions he warmed to his task and issued a full-blown, and rather fearsome set of 'TERMS AND REGULATIONS for the Chauffeurs to THEIR MAJESTIES THE KING AND QUEEN'. Starting with the wages which, at three pounds a week, were exceptionally high for any servant at the beginning of the century, he went on to detail times and procedures for daily duties and the Sunday inspection by himself. After spelling out the routine in quasi-military terms, this Major-General betrayed the natural anxiety of any commander to know the position of his troops. 'When a car is ordered away a telegram is to be sent reporting its safe arrival or otherwise.' One gets the impression that the sender of the telegram would have had a bit of explaining to do if it were 'otherwise'.

Comprehensive though the instructions are, Sir Henry clearly felt that there was more to be said, and he added a sort of embryonic Highway Code. 'It is,' he wrote, 'desired to particularly impress the necessity for turns to be taken most carefully and steadily. When the road is straight and clear speed may be put on accordingly, but no risk whatever must be run to endanger the occupants of the car.'

He might well have laid down his pen and leaned back with the satisfaction of a job well done. But no, there was one final injunction which he could not help adding: 'The cars are always to go very slowly in and out of the Mews.'

In spite of the meticulously detailed orders, the man responsible for seeing that they were scrupulously observed, the Superintendent of the Royal Mews, found it necessary to issue a pronunciamento of his own. 'With reference to Clause Nine of the Chauffeurs' Terms and Regulations, it is perfectly understood thereby that the Chauffeurs are responsible in every way for the cleanliness of their cars, the washing only being done for them,' he wrote in a style tolerably well imitating the sonorous periods of the original. But his exasperation was too much for him. 'It does not mean that all the work of cleaning has to be done by the washers while the chauffeurs idle away the time with their hands in their pockets,' he added, spoiling it all.

Whether the Palace was having servant trouble, or whether it was that the traditional system was too inflexible to adapt itself, is uncertain. But, for whatever reason, it was decided in 1905 that chauffeurs for the royal cars should be constables of the Metropolitan Police, specially selected by the Commissioner. The two retired Generals no doubt sighed with relief that henceforward they would be dealing with men who understood discipline, but machines are not susceptible to discipline and the mechanical problems remained. While King Edward used Daimlers for official business and Mercedes for private journeys, Queen Alexandra used Wolseleys, and it was to the London agents for Wolseley that the Palace appealed for help. The manager of the Testing and Repairs Department was C. W. Stamper, and he spent three months of the early summer instructing the new chauffeurs 'in the management of the cars they were to control'.

It was about this time that Letzer departed, and either this precipitated a crisis or it was a remarkable coincidence that Sir Henry Ewart turned up at ten o'clock one morning at the offices of the firm for which Stamper worked and demanded that Stamper and one of the new chauffeurs should immediately take him for a drive. On the journey round Soho the Crown Equerry offered Stamper the job of 'His Majesty's motor expert and engineer, and to take charge of the royal cars at once.'

Stamper very reasonably pointed out that it would be unfair to chuck in his present job without giving his employers proper notice, but, when approached by Sir Henry, the managing director gave his immediate consent and by lunchtime on the same day Stamper was installed in the royal Mews. Early in the afternoon he climbed up beside the chauffeur and drove round to the Terrace Entrance of Buckingham Palace, ready to take the King to Sandown Park races. King Edward was standing chatting to a couple of members of the Household, and he smiled a welcome as Stamper clambered down and took off his hat.

'So you are the new engineer,' said the King.

'Yes, Your Majesty.'

King Edward pointed to the car.

'This is a nice car and a very powerful one. It's a 40-horsepower Mercedes. I haven't had it long. I suppose it's powerful enough to go anywhere, isn't it?'

Stamper was a cautious man, and he never made a promise or a statement which he could not substantiate. So instead of saying 'yes' and leaving it at that, he firmly but tactfully qualified his reply.

'It's a good powerful make, Your Majesty.'

But the King pressed him harder. 'I suppose you can guarantee our never having any stops?'

'I can't do that, Your Majesty, but if we should stop, I can very quickly put it right so that there's no time lost.'

That short conversation enabled each to get the measure of the other. Until the King's death five years later they saw one another almost every day. Except when he was travelling by train or yacht it was the King's habit to go for a drive, usually in the afternoon after a morning's work, and invariably Stamper occupied the front seat beside the chauffeur. On these outings they were accompanied by Caesar, the King's much-loved, much-spoilt and disobedient fox terrier. Many a time Stamper would have to retrieve the mud-encrusted animal from a ditch where he had been seeking out the local rats and cradle him in his arms for the drive home from a picnic. Caesar did not care for being clasped in the arms of the 'motor expert' and always tried to wriggle free. Normally he would ride with his master on the back seat and he resented being banished to the front compartment. On one occasion he was particularly wet and slimy and managed to slip out of Stamper's grasp and take a flying leap out of the car. He was in fact tethered by his lead but the people in the following car did not know this and were horrified to see the King's beloved dog hurtle apparently to his death. But even before the lead restrained him Stamper neatly fielded the little bundle of off-white fur.

It was said of Queen Victoria that, when attending the opera, she would walk to the front of the royal box, acknowledge the acclaim of the audience, and then sit down without looking behind her, secure in the knowledge that somebody would have placed a chair there. This complete confidence that nothing would go wrong with royal arrangements was inherited in full measure by her son. Motor cars, King Edward felt, were for travelling about in, and if they did not fulfill this function it was a personal affront, an outrage. On the rare occasions – and they were surprisingly rare – that a car broke down, he would utter the chilling words 'This should not be.'

King Edward's rages were proverbial, the blue eyes flashing fire, the royal 'r's rolling like thunder. Stamper experienced a few of these, and very terrifying they were, but they were soon over and, at least as far as the King was concerned, completely forgotten. Sometimes, however, he used gentle irony instead. 'He would,' wrote Stamper, 'show his displeasure by assuming an air of the most complete resignation. Instead, perhaps, of upbraiding me if I lost the way, he would question me quietly so as to ascertain what was wrong, gravely deplore the way in which Misfortune singled him out for her victim, and then settle himself gently in his corner, as if resigning himself to his fate.'

Once a car carrying his Equerry broke down while following the King from Biarritz to an official engagement at Pau, and the King was reduced to scanning the hotel visitor's book to find a stand-in. The delay was caused by magneto trouble and, if they had been directed at the car instead of at Stamper, the sparks which flew would have been quite enough to keep it going. But Stamper was a clever mechanic and he usually managed to avoid trouble. Often if some minor defect appeared while they were on a journey he would effect a repair without stopping. He was an agile little man and he would lie along the wing and adjust the carburettor while the chauffeur kept the car bucketing along at forty miles an hour, its royal occupant unaware that anything untoward was happening. Only once did Stamper record the final ignominy, when, wind as he might, a royal car could not be started at Newmarket station and His Majesty was reduced to taking a cab.

Although he regarded mechanical breakdown as a personal insult, King Edward was extraordinarily philosophical about tyre trouble and would stroll about quite happily while Stamper and the chauffeur changed a tyre. In the early days it was always a struggle, but in 1907 the cars were fitted with detachable rims, and thereafter the time of the hold-up was reduced to something like a racing pitstop, the record being seven minutes.

Detachable rims were not the only modification made to the royal cars. Originally they were limousines, that is the passenger compartment was closed, with the front seats in the open. King Edward had the limousine roofs adapted so that the back halves folded down – in other words, the limousines were converted to landaulettes. The King, who liked fresh air, usually drove with the back open, but once, when he was driving in procession through Manchester, it was a chilly day and he kept the hood up. This was just as well, because if the hood had been lowered one of the accompanying cars would not have been able to conform. The cars had come up from London by train and one of the interior hood struts had been broken so that the corner sagged. Stamper had no time to make a new hinged strut but he cut a length of wood to prop up the drooping leather. It was a Sunday and he could not find a shop open where he could buy a length of dark blue cloth to cover the strut. However, the cars were garaged in the fire station and the ingenious Stamper had the bright idea of buying a pair of trousers from one of the firemen, whose uniforms exactly matched the cloth interior of the hood.

Stamper was always worried when the cars travelled by train, and on one occasion in Paris his fears were justified. The car was loaded on to an open wagon, and Stamper asked for a receptacle into which to drain the petrol tank. This the railway authorities officiously refused, and insisted that the petrol should be allowed to flow on to the floor of the wagon and so on to the line. Stamper had to comply, and was just sheeting the car up when it burst into flames. His hands were burned as he plied the fire extinguisher, and a porter emptied a bucket of water over him, but they managed to get the fire out before the car became a write-off. It was, however, sufficiently badly damaged to spend a fortnight at a coachbuilder's, and a replacement had to be sent from England. This was no simple task before the days of drive-on, drive-off ferries. A special platform had to be built on the deck of the Folkestone – Boulogne packet, and when the boat entered the harbour at three o'clock in the morning Stamper thought the tarpaulin-covered excrescence on the deck looked like a haystack.

The King was in the habit of making at least two trips abroad each year, to Biarritz and to Marienbad, and Stamper and the cars always went too, for after a morning's work His Majesty liked to go for a drive in the country and have one of his gargantuan meals *al fresco*. It was Stamper's responsibility to set out the various hampers for these leisurely feasts, and the King always made sure that there was plenty of food for him and the chauffeurs. While they were eating their picnic the King would usually take a stroll in a nearby wood and almost invariably come back without Caesar. 'You go and call him, Stamper,' he would say. 'He'll recognize your voice.' Probably Caesar did, but he seldom took much notice.

On one of his Continental trips the King met his nephew, the Kaiser, who had just acquired a fascinating accessory for his car. The Kaiser was notoriously jealous of Uncle Bertie, who, in his turn, was determined to keep up with the Hohenzollerns. The Kaiser had a new toy so the King must have one like it. This accessory was a horn – no simple bulb or klaxon but a four-note bugle which Stamper held across his knees (when he was not clutching Caesar) like a guard on a stage-coach with his blunderbuss. When necessary he would raise it to his lips and trill away as if playing a cornet. The King was the archetype, if not actually the prototype, of the backseat driver, and he was always abjuring Stamper to blow the horn. On days when the window behind the driver was raised the King would tap on the glass to attract Stamper's attention and then distend his cheeks and hold his hands out in front of his mouth, miming the action. The sight of this elderly Pan playing his imaginary pipes made Stamper smile, and the King would burst into his deep-throated laughter.

Some of the royal desire for one-up-man-ship over the Kaiser rubbed off on Stamper, but it was not until after the King's death that the opportunity arose. The Kaiser was staying at Buckingham Palace and asked that Stamper should accompany the chauffeur driving him in one of the royal cars to Stoke Poges. When they got back the Kaiser remarked that it was one of the pleasantest drives he had ever had, and asked Stamper what make of car it was. Stamper had to admit that it was a German Mercedes. 'Why,' said the Kaiser in surprise, 'I haven't got a car in the whole of my stud that rides so easily and travels so quietly. Now why is that?'

Stamper proceeded to blind him with science so that the Kaiser had to call over his Ober-Hofmarschall to hear all about the mounting of the body on the chassis. Stamper mentioned something to do with the chain-cases, and the Kaiser interrupted him. 'But surely this is a gear-driven car?'

'No, Your Imperial Majesty. It is driven by chains.'

The Kaiser was astonished. 'I've got several chain-driven cars and I can't hear myself speak in them.'

With his withered arm the Kaiser could not, of course, drive a car himself, but he was an interested passenger. One day he was being driven along a deserted country road at a spanking pace when another chauffeur-driven car containing an Englishman emerged from a road running at right-angles. The two heavy cars weaved round one another, swaying on their cart-springs, and finally drew up without colliding. The two passengers hopped out to congratulate one another on their narrow escape from death and the Englishman was dumb-founded to find himself shaking hands with the Kaiser. Some years later, in a dug-out near Ypres, he reflected ruefully that if the chauffeurs had not been skilful enough to avoid disaster a much greater catastrophe might never have taken place.

Stamper may have been gleefully exaggerating the difficulties of getting the setting of the body on the chassis just right, but it was an operation which provided plenty of opportunities for error. Every single year the body of each car was removed from the chassis and sent to the coachbuilder for painting and varnishing. While this was being done the engines and chassis were being completely overhauled in the mews at Buckingham Palace. As soon as one was finished Stamper would take it for a test drive of a couple of hundred miles, mounted on a soapbox bolted to the chassis. Only when he was satisfied that it was in perfect mechanical condition would he allow the body to be put back. These overhauls were done in April every year and were finished in three weeks. This was the time when the King went cruising in the royal yacht, but for the rest of the year the cars were in almost constant use and Stamper had reason to be proud of the fact that, except for routine maintenance, they were never off the road between annual overhauls.

The development of motoring, as well as that of cars, progressed very quickly in the first decade of the twentieth century. From being an adventurous alternative to a horse-drawn vehicle for short trips, the car became the main means of transport, and the King loved to be driven for quite long distances on pleasure outings. He would think nothing of going seventy miles to a favourite picnic site and returning after lunch – or whenever Caesar could be found. During the month he spent at Biarritz he would cover over two thousand miles, sometimes nearer three, and as early as 1906 he was boasting about touching sixty miles per hour.

In England the twenty miles per hour speed limit was enforced long after cars were capable of travelling quite fast with safety, and it was only the fact that the royal cars (except the little Renault which the King used when shopping incognito in London) had no number plates which saved them being stopped many a time. Once the King was returning from Newmarket and Stamper was told to instruct the chauffeur to 'let her out' on the long straight of Six Mile Bottom. Many of the race-goers, confident that the police would not set a trap for the King, careered along after him. Their confidence in the royal inviolability was not misplaced and His Majesty's car thundered on while the followers, including the Crown Equerry, were bagged by the vigilant constables.

While the royal cars were instantly recognized in England because they carried no number plates, this was not so abroad. In 1907 Their Majesties paid a State visit to Paris, and Stamper, who had never been there before, was sent ahead to familiarize himself with the routes. 'Parisian traffic,' he soon discovered, 'is not regulated as is the traffic of London. A certain disregard of order and convenience prevails.' What he did not realize was that when a gendarme blew his whistle and pointed with his baton the car was supposed to stop there and then. Stamper drew tidily into the kerb and the angry gendarme had to run after him and jump on the running board to demand why the car had no number plate. Stamper haughtily pointed out that it belonged to the King of England.

This made the policeman angrier still. He was not, his faith, going to have his leg pulled by any supercilious Englishman. Stamper did not get the finer points of what the gendarme was saying, but the gist of it was obvious. It was the French equivalent of the dreaded phrase, 'You come along with me.'

At the police station they flatly refused to believe Stamper's story. Preposterous, they said. If the King of England were in Paris the police would be the first people to know. In vain Stamper expostulated that the King had not yet arrived and that he, Stamper was a forerunner. Still stark disbelief. Stamper then played his trump card. 'Telephone the British Embassy,' he commanded. This produced the opposite effect to that which he intended. The police flatly refused. They were not going to make fools of themselves by ringing up the British Embassy with a cock and bull story like that. They would never live it down. But the cheek of the man! You had to laugh.

Finally Stamper did what he ought to have done in the first place. With his talk of Kings and Embassies he had overdone the name-dropping. Now he mentioned a senior detective whom he had met at Biarritz the year before. That did the trick. A quick telephone call and Stamper was free. But his ordeal was not quite over. Next day he was mortified to see the story emblazoned across every Paris newspaper and some English ones as well. Really, it was not at all funny.

The King, however, thought otherwise, and when Stamper met him at the Gare du Nord two days later he greeted him with a cheery, 'Well, Stamper, I see they've let you out.'

The King and Queen then got into the Ambassador's car and were driven away through crowds yelling their welcome. A few seconds later the royal car swung out of the station yard and the crowd recognized the car which had become famous because of its lack of number plates. They set up a friendly shout and for Stamper the incident closed with, ringing in his ears, the stirring cry of 'Vive le chauffeur!'

But this heady stuff was not quite enough to dispel his distrust of foreigners. 'It was not,' he wrote, 'easy to forget the lesson of 1906.' This took place at Marienbad where Stamper arrived with a brand new Mercedes. In his usual lordly way he told the garage to produce a man to clean the car. 'Presently the fellow appeared. I showed him the car and told him to wash it very carefully, and to put a few drops of paraffin in the water he used, but on no account to put any of the oil on the car itself.'

Whether it was excess of zeal or whether it was because of Stamper's inadequate mastery of German, the cleaner disregarded the instructions and sploshed paraffin all over the car, neatly removing the thick coat of varnish. When Stamper returned from dinner at the hotel he immediately gave tongue, and 'those whom my ejaculations of dismay did not bring upon the scene came running in answer to my cries of anger.' There was no time either to have that car revarnished or to send for another one, so there was nothing for it but for Stamper and the chauffeur to set to and polish it themselves. After a day and a half's hard work they had restored most of its lustre with a polish which Stamper mixed himself. Maddeningly, he does not tell us its composition. He does, however, inform us that the cleaner was found to have had no previous experience of cars, 'but was really a greengrocer.'

It was not until the early 1930s that it became general for cars to be sprayed with cellulose, and right up until that time chauffeurs suffered from having to deal with paint and varnish. The varnish had nothing like the hard shell of cellulose and was very easily scratched. It could even be damaged by pressing on it with a finger, as Stamper discovered one wet day in Cambridge. He was on his way to Sandringham and he had stopped for lunch, parking the car in the hotel yard. When he came out he was horrified to see that somebody had scrawled *graffiti* in the mud on the high back panel. It turned out that it was the work of an undergraduate who had recognized the car as being a royal one because of its distinctive plum colour and lack of number plates. The message was quite an innocuous one, of the 'good old Teddy' variety, but if it had been the vilest insult it could not have stirred Stamper more. He was absolutely outraged that His Majesty's car should be defaced, and by an educated Englishman. What made it even worse, if that were possible, was that the young man was actually a car-owner himself. Stamper 'rated him fiercely', and he was duly penitent. When the car was washed the writing stood out just as clearly, indented in the delicate varnish. Fortunately it was winter and driving on the untarred roads of the time the summer dust was replaced by fine mud thrown up by the wheels whose mudguards swept up so gracefully but ineffectually at the back, so that almost as soon as a journey started the message was shrouded. But Stamper did not have an easy moment until the following April, when the car was due for its annual revarnish. It was unlikely that the King would take it into his head to walk round the back of the car, but you never knew. It was an anxious time.

An undergraduate's finger was by no means the most dangerous weapon to attack the King's car. As Stamper put it, 'Both at home and abroad His Majesty met with the same treatment at the hands of mischievous children as was meted out to any and every motorist. Stones and other missiles were flung at us many a time, and once or twice they have passed into the car and narrowly missed the King. 'Other occupants of the car had been struck more than once. No glass was ever broken, but the panels were dented time and again.'

As he points out, there was nothing anti-monarchical about these attacks. Cars were noisy, smelly, they raised an intolerable cloud of dust or mud, according to season, they killed dogs and chickens and they frightened horses. No wonder they were unpopular. The King was well aware of this, and being a most considerate man, he always insisted that his cars should go very slowly through villages to cause as little inconvenience as possible, and he was proud of the fact that no animal was ever hurt by his cars. Sometimes things were thrown at him with happier intention, and once a bunch of flowers landed in the royal lap. The car was travelling slowly enough for the King to congratulate the thrower on the accuracy of her aim.

But it was not only the inhabitants of remote villages who were hostile to cars. The redoubtable Sir Dighton Probyn turned his face firmly against these new-fangled machines. 'I would rather go with my horses, Sir,' he informed the King when invited to accompany His Majesty on a tour of the Sandringham estate. 'I don't like cars very much.' When the King pressed him he went on protesting. 'I shall be there as soon as you,' he assured His Majesty. Then, pointing to the sleek and beautiful animals standing waiting with his carriage he added, 'I bred them myself, Sir,' as if that clinched the matter. Founder of the famous Indian cavalry regiment which bore his name though he was, holder of the Victoria Cross though he was, close friend of the King though he was, Sir Dighton still failed to carry his point. 'You'll have to get used to the cars,' His Majesty told him bleakly.

It was with great satisfaction that Stamper observed at Balmoral a couple of years later that Sir Dighton had a car, and of the horses no more was heard.

While Stamper's main task was to keep the cars in good running order, he gradually assumed another heavy responsibility as well. That

was route-planning and navigation. The King was a stickler for
punctuality, and anything which disrupted his timetable was apt to
spark off an explosion of rage. One disastrous day he set out from
Marienbad to lunch at Karlsbad. The previous year they had entered
the town through narrow, congested streets and Sir Stanley Clarke
suggested that if they turned off a few miles earlier they could enter the
town at a junction quite near their destination. Accordingly Stamper
worked it all out. Sir Stanley was a little anxious, and, just as they were
approaching the turning, he asked Stamper to pass him the map. He
took a quick look and handed it back. Then, not entirely convinced, he
asked for it again. Stamper once more gave it to him, and precisely at
that moment a turning appeared. Stamper was not sure whether this
was the one they wanted but he took a chance. By the way he snatched
the map back from Sir Stanley the royal backseat driver sensed that it
was not the right way, and immediately gave tongue. 'You're wrong,
Stamper, you're wrong. You'll land me in a farmyard.'

The same thought had crossed Stamper's mind, and he scanned the
map frantically to find an escape. To his immense relief there was one,
in the shape of a lane. Thankfully he told the chauffeur to take it, and
sank back in his seat, congratulating himself on having saved the day.

But not for long. The lane got steeper and steeper, until the Mercedes
was grinding up in first gear. Above the sound of the labouring engine
and the clanking of the chains could be heard the explosion of royal
rage with its chorus of 'You're wrong, Stamper, you're wrong! You'll
land me in a farmyard, I know you will.'

And when, in due course, Stamper did just that, the King's fury
reached its crescendo. More to get away than anything, Stamper got
down and went to question a man standing nearby. 'Where has the fool
gone?' the King roared at the chauffeur. 'He can't speak a word of
German. Why doesn't he bring the man to me. Go and fetch him.'

The chauffeur would have been delighted to comply but the car was
standing at an awkward angle on the crest of a slope. He could not, he
felt, safely leave it. He imparted this information to the King – a brave
thing to do.

'Do you refuse to do as I tell you?' thundered his royal master.

'Yes, Your Majesty. I daren't leave the car.'

He braced himself for the onslaught, but before it could be launched
the King caught sight of his detective, who had dismounted from the
following car and was standing beside the wagon. 'What's the use of

hiding behind that cart?' bellowed the King. 'Come and help.'

But by this time Stamper had returned, more hot and bothered than ever, with the tidings that the only thing to do was to turn round and retrace their tyremarks.

The King took this in the biggest possible way, and it was only Sir Stanley Clarke's courageous intervention, shouldering the entire blame for having taken the map at the critical moment, which diverted the King's attention from the unhappy Stamper.

With a final rumble of 'Everybody else can get to Karlsbad in fifty minutes but I – I can't get there under two hours,' the incident closed. But there was an echo a year later when, bowling along the main road, they drove past the turning. 'Remember that road, Stamper?' the King asked with a smile. Stamper did.

While the King was always exasperated when, for any reason, a journey took longer than expected, he was, equally, delighted when it took less time. 'Fine run, Stamper,' he would say approvingly, 'fine run.' Forty miles per hour seems to have been the normal cruising speed on the open road, but when there was no particular reason to hurry the King was content to be driven at a modest fifteen when pottering along lanes. No concessions were made to the weather, and Stamper records without comment that when he took the King for a drive on New Year's Day 1908, 'there had been a fall of snow overnight and it was freezing hard.' Royal cars went out even when fog was so thick that a chauffeur had to walk in front with a lamp, and one year getting the King's car to Biarritz entailed driving from Paris with four inches of snow on the road.

The King himself made the journeys to Biarritz and Marienbad by train, but in the last years of his reign his cars went by road, covering distances in a day which would even now be regarded as quite considerable. In 1907 Stamper and Payne, the chauffeur who most often drove the King, did the four hundred miles from Marienbad to Coblenz between six in the morning and nightfall, eating as they went along and sliding across to change seats without stopping.

But a drive of even more heroic proportions took place two years later. The King was due in Marienbad on 10 August, and Stamper was anxious to have a clear day before his arrival to service the car. Accordingly he left London on 5 August, but there were several delays so he and Payne did not get away from Antwerp until midday. They stopped in Turnhout and stocked up with bread, cold meat and fruit, enough to keep them going for the rest of the journey. Then they set off for Austria.

They made good time and they were already running into Cologne when the light began to fade. They stopped outside the city, lit the acetelyne gas for the great brass headlights, and hastened on again. From past experience they knew that the road ran through lush and lovely country but the orchards and vineyards, the spreading meadows, the woods, streams and mountains were masked from them by the darkness of a moonless night. All they could see was the narrow ribbon of road, its white surface harshly tossing back the glare of the headlights until their eyes ached.

Before they left the Rhine they filled up with petrol, both the tank and a spare can, at about midnight. But the garageman in the little town was the last living creature they saw before dawn. As they sped on they passed through villages where the windows were tightly shuttered, the streets were deserted and the only signs of life were the barking of dogs aroused by the Mercedes thundering past. Stamper drove through the night, and urged Payne to get what sleep he could. But the swaying and jolting of the high and heavy car would have made it difficult to doze even without the rush of the night air through the open driving compartment. Several times Payne protested that Stamper was driving too fast, and once he bent forward and cupped a match in his hands to read the speedometer. Probably on the whole trip they never exceeded fifty miles an hour, but the height above the ground, the almost total lack of protection from the wind, the noise of the engine and the bouncing of the narrow tyres on the uneven road made it seem much more. Payne announced that he was far too busy praying to think of going to sleep.

As the sun rose Stamper surrendered the wheel to him, and plied him with food which he munched as he drove. In daylight they travelled more slowly, because they had to observe the speed limits in towns and villages, in some of which the limit was as low as five miles per hour. When they attempted to exceed that the angry shouts of the inhabitants warned them to slow down. Many of the bridges they came to had toll-bars. These had been raised during the night, but in the daytime drivers had to stop to pay their dues. In 1909 cars were still comparatively rare, as most people travelled by train, so that on a long journey one always had to allow for lengthy hold-ups at level crossings.

They took it in turns to drive, and Stamper's last spell came to an end twenty miles short of their destination. Choosing a straight stretch of road he let the speed fall then raising himself against the steering wheel he allowed Payne to slip in behind him. Stamper snuggled his weary body down in the passenger seat and, in spite of the noise and discomfort, sank into a sleep of exhaustion. Payne was in no better shape, and began nodding over the wheel.

Suddenly Stamper awoke, alerted by the clairvoyance of extreme fatigue. Payne was asleep with his eyes open. And the Mercedes was heading straight for a massive tree. Stamper grabbed the wheel and heaved the great car back on to the road. His yell roused Payne and the shock was so great that it banished all drowsiness.

In the mid-afternoon of 8 August they came to Marienbad, six hundred and more miles from their starting point twenty-five hours before. Their eyes red-rimmed, their haggard unshaven cheeks thickly powdered with dust, they slept until late on the following day. But by the time the King arrived on the 10 August the car was spotless, the boots and leggings gleaming. Caesar came out of the station first, tugging at the lead held by the sergeant-footman. The little dog greeted Payne and Stamper with a joyous bark and jumped on to his accustomed seat, waiting impatiently for his master who emerged smiling from the station.

'Well, Stamper, did you have a good trip?'

'Yes, thank you, Your Majesty.'

'That's right.'

Three weeks later they made the return journey, at the same forced pace. The car ran faultlessly, as usual, and, to Stamper's amazement, on neither trip did they have a single puncture. Again Stamper drove all night and this time Payne slept soundly beside him. They had had a busy three weeks and had hardly had a chance to recover from their outward marathon. At one o'clock in the morning they came to the white-painted stones which marked the road's edge where it ran along the bank of the mighty Rhine. For a moment Stamper's attention wandered and the car strayed towards the verge. He yanked at the wheel and the car swerved so violently that Payne was amost flung out. That night he slept no more.

But when daylight came fatigue overcame fear, and Payne slumbered. They drove through Antwerp with him lolling back with his mouth open, sprawling half out of the car. The passers-by paused to giggle and point to the big travel-stained limousine with its little driver hunched over the wheel and beside him the chauffeur, apparently dead drunk.

It is doubtful if King Edward ever knew of these epic journeys, and if he had known he would probably not have thought them anything out of the ordinary, so immense was his own energy. In the last weeks of his life, when he was already far from well, he made the journey, by train and ship, from Biarritz to London, arriving at Buckingham Palace at six o'clock in the evening, having been travelling non-stop for nineteen hours. That evening he went to the opera.

Three years after the King's death Stamper published the memoirs of his royal employment. The book was written with the help of Dornford Yates, and it is both smooth and vivid. It gives a lively picture of what it was like to be a chauffeur in the Edwardian age, and indeed it is probably the best picture which could be given, for it is written by the employee of the man who gave the age its name. From its pages King Edward emerges as benign, genial, an impatient perfectionist larger than life, served by devoted and discreet men. Stamper preserved his discretion to the end. No hint is given of the King's private life and, fascinating though the book is, it is entirely bland. The only sensational thing about it is the title, *What I know*.

What Stamper knew he was not telling, and the title is wildly misleading. But when, in 1913, the next king, George v saw it displayed in the window of a Piccadilly bookshop as he was driving past, he growled, 'Ha! I wonder what Stamper knows about my father that *I* don't!'

9

'Abroad, and See New Sights'

Humphrey Gifford

Before the First World War, foreign travel for pleasure was the prerogative of the well-to-do. Any young man with *wanderlust* but no money had either to join the armed services or find some job which would post him abroad, or perhaps take him abroad for comparatively short periods. Many chauffeuring jobs came into this last category and were eagerly sought after by adventurous youths who wished to spread their wings farther than across a factory bench.

One whose imagination was fired by the romance and glamour of foreign travel, Cecil Paull, wrote as follows: 'Some lads wished to be engine drivers. I wanted to be a real top Rolls-Royce chauffeur to the best Society and with them travel the world, something I had no hope of doing otherwise. How this all came to pass is like a fairy tale.'

This ambition was formed when he was nine years old, in 1913. The father of one of his school friends was a chauffeur, and one day Cecil Paull went round to see them. Standing in the mews was the first Rolls-Royce the boy had ever seen, '. . . a beautiful Silver Ghost named Blue Bird.' He was enthralled by the beauty of the car and the pictures it conjured up of freedom and adventure. During a long and happy working life – he did not retire until he was nearly seventy – his ambitions were amply fulfilled, and he travelled all over Europe and toured in Morocco, and the United States, also having a three-month spell in the Bahamas.

Seven years before Cecil Paull gazed wide-eyed at 'Blue Bird' another lad was having his first taste of Continental touring. He had become a chauffeur at the age of seventeen and a year later his employer told him to drive the car to Marseilles; the employer himself was travelling there by yacht with his wife. The chauffeur had never even been as far as London before, and of course he spoke not one word of any foreign language. It may seem that the employer was highly irresponsible, but possibly he had complete confidence in this exceptional young man, who overcame all the difficulties, geographical, mechanical and linguistic, and arrived in Marseilles a day ahead of schedule. When he had serviced the car, he spent the remaining time not as might be expected of an eighteen-year-old on his first visit to France, but in learning the route from the docks to the main road he was to take on leaving Marseilles.

It would be interesting to know whether either the chauffeur or the employer had read the *Continental Touring Guide for Motorists Abroad*, which *The Car Illustrated* published that same year. 'A chauffeur with a knowledge of French,' it begins, 'is always of great assistance, even if the tourist himself knows foreign languages well. Otherwise his employer will always have to translate for him, and this is often inconvenient.' It is quite clear that the writer of the Guide never visualized eighteen-year-old non-French speaking chauffeurs careering across France on their own. Much of the advice to the employer could only be taken if he too were travelling in the car. The Guide turns to the chauffeur's duties – 'Keep a firm hand on him, but treat him well. It is to the employer's profit that he should be kept in good health and temper.' The words might have been lifted from a guide for plantation owners on the treatment of slaves, written some two hundred years before.

'Touring,' warns the Guide sternly, 'engenders sluggishness and too easy-going habits. Let him see before starting that a high standard of work will be expected of him, *and prevent him scorching*.' Possibly the word 'scorching' started an association of ideas, for the Guide went on to insist that 'he fits himself out neatly and tidily, and that his clothing is appropriate. Otherwise he may get sunstroke in Italy and pneumonia on the Swiss passes. This is awkward for his master.' Not all that convenient for the chauffeur either, one imagines.

The author of the Guide unbends a little at one point where he remarks that one of the advantages of a chauffeur who speaks French is that 'he amuses himself more easily when off duty'. But, lest he should be suspected of tolerance amounting to weakness, the author hastens to imply that there are strict limits to the form of the amusement. 'If possible avoid taking a chauffeur whose manners are bad and natural instincts low,' he warns severely.

Curiously enough, the same Guide goes on to give some very sensible advice to the chauffeur himself. 'Do your best to scare animals and poultry away from the course of the car. The inhabitants regard it as a friendly act if done in an obviously friendly way. Some motorists use a little stick wherewith to pat the bonnet and produce a metallic sound. If you break down in a town or village and have to repair, for instance, a tyre, do not assume a hostile attitude towards the crowd of curiosity mongers. Get them to give room and air, but do not push.' Suddenly the Guide relaxes and allows a trace of humour to creep in. 'Some of them,' it continues, 'will help, often for the honour, and it is not unpleasant to get someone else to do the pumping up.' It might even be necessary, if the chauffeur has disregarded the advice about clothing and is suffering from sunstroke and pneumonia.

In spite of the hazards, the lure of foreign travel did much to ensure that chauffeuring was a trade which attracted the enterprising and the adventurous and those who were not afraid of taking responsibility. Consequently chauffeurs tended to be a slightly better type than men of similar education who were content with other trades. Many, like Cecil Paull, found complete fulfillment in the job, but few can have found that it exceeded their expectations to the degree which Martin Harper did.

Harper was engaged by the young Lionel de Rothschild and they were both twenty-three when they set out together in 1903 to drive a 40-horsepower Mercedes to Rome. They took it in turns to drive, and everywhere they stopped the car aroused considerable interest. Foreigners were well used to eccentric English travellers complaining about the food and scattering golden sovereigns. But this outlandish machine, accompanied by two equally outlandish figures clad in ankle-length mackintoshes and with their goggles pushed up on to their little round caps to disclose white circles round their eyes in otherwise mud-encrusted faces – this was something quite new. They crowded round in friendly curiosity.

One man who was not quite so friendly was a carter whom they followed for some way after leaving Genoa. The cart was loaded with marble from the quarries at Carrara and its progress was very slow. Lionel de Rothschild was driving, and he gave a little toot on the bulb horn as a request to the carter to pull over. But the carter did not see it that way. For two or three thousand years marble had been brought down this track – did not the whole mountainside glitter with white dust, like snow, to prove it? And now here was this frightful machine, quivering with evil intent, challenging his right of passage. An instinct born of ancient race-memory prompted him to jump down and advance upon the offending vehicle.

When the carter drew a long knife from his belt, Harper and de Rothschild reacted immediately. The driver revved up the engine and let in the clutch while the chauffeur stretched his arm over the back of the seat and grabbed the jack handle which, being needed so frequently, was kept ready on the floor. With the smooth tyres slithering from side to side on the narrow, rutted mountain track they just managed to squeeze past with Harper brandishing his jack handle and the carter screaming with fear and fury.

This exhibition of what Harper later described as 'a remarkably good piece of pilotage' gave him great confidence in his employer's driving ability until, on a later trip, de Rothschild fell sleep at the wheel and turned the car over into a potato field. This was the ignominious end to an example of the favourite pastime of enterprising motorists – trying to race a train, in this case the Engadine Express to St Moritz.

The 40-horsepower Mercedes had by this time been exchanged for a bigger one, of 60-horsepower, and the mishap in no way diminished the young men's enthusiasm for Continental travel. In one year they crossed the Channel nine times.

On a trip to Spain Harper fell ill. He was not the first – nor would he be the last – Englishman to contract 'Madrid tummy', but he quickly recovered under the skilful nursing of de Rothschild's mother who insisted on personally preparing the broth for the sick chauffeur and shooing her son away from his bedside on the grounds that he 'was not in a fit state to talk cars'.

Another of these big 60-horsepower Mercedes was owned by Lord Northcliffe. He and his chauffeur, whose name was Pine, collected it from the factory in Stuttgart and left to keep an appointment in Paris. On the way the car developed trouble and Pine had to drop the bottom half of the gearbox, catching the oil in a collapsible canvas bucket. Lord Northcliffe stood beside him with his watch in his hand, but Pine knew his job and very soon the gearbox was assembled again, the oil poured back, and the journey resumed. On arrival in Paris, in time for this important appointment, Pine was rewarded with a sum equalling a week's wages. As he was in any case highly paid, this was considerable. However, although Lord Northcliffe was both kind and generous, he was an exacting employer, and Pine knew that if ever he were to be involved in an accident, no matter whether it was his fault or not, he would be instantly dismissed.

Lord Northcliffe was intensely interested in cars, and in spite of his unease about accidents, he had a great respect for Pine, often consulting him about the reports on cars to appear in the *Daily Mail*.

Another chauffeur who was very much at home on the Continent was Teddy Stephens who had taken over from his brother as chauffeur to the second Lord Montagu. He is remembered as being 'a marvellous man to take abroad'. He could speak French, which was a great help, particularly as his pronunciation, though not easily understood in Northern France, approximated very closely to the accents of the Midi. He always made sure that no luggage was left behind, saw to it that the car was readily available and not hemmed in when garaged overnight, and had an encyclopedic memory for the places to obtain good food and cheap petrol.

During the First World War he served with Lord Montagu in India and remained with the family until his death in 1932.

Englishmen of the leisured classes had for long been accustomed to visiting the Continent, and in the eighteenth century the Grand Tour, sometimes lasting several years, was considered part of a gentleman's education. There are many tales of hair-raising adventure, of highwaymen, of coach and carriage accidents, of filthy inns and rascally landlords. But the coming of railways altered the whole concept of a Continental tour. Far more people travelled, but they saw far less on the way. This pattern of travel changed only slowly with the coming of the motor car. Train remained the normal means of getting to a distant destination and was by far the best, being fast, comfortable and reliable. The fashion was to stay in places like Cannes, Monte Carlo or Biarritz towards the end of the winter and to remain in England at high summer. Unless the traveller was an enthusiastic motorist he would infinitely prefer the luxury of an express train to jolting for days down execrable roads in a snowstorm. Far better to go by train and hire a car on arrival.

On the whole, English travellers were slow to follow King Edward's example of having his own car driven out to meet him when he reached his destination. Consequently, up until the First World War, driving long distances on the Continent was regarded as high adventure.

Could it be that it was King Edward VII who first discovered the suitability of the yachting cap for open-car motoring? He is seen here being driven in, or rather on, a 1901 22-hp Daimler by the father of the present Lord Montagu of Beaulieu.

King Edward VII's first car, a 6-hp Daimler, with his chauffeur Letzer at the wheel.

Whether the chauffeur is touching his cap or scratching his ear is uncertain, but it is clear that he is not opening the door of Lilly Langtry's electric brougham for her.

Vesta Tilley, not to be outdone, had an up-to-date steering wheel rather than an old-fashioned tiller.

aisev's Cup. 1907
Daimler.

Oliver Bush driving the Kaiserpreis Daimler of 1907. He acted as chauffeur to King Alfonso of Spain when he visited England.

Zélélé, the Abyssinian chauffeur at the start of his long career with the Marquis de Dion.

Two Panhards and a Mercedes of Lord Northcliffe's stable at Sutton Place.

Lord Northcliffe hovers impatiently over his chauffeur Pine who is making one of the frequent tyre changes. Another discomfort which early chauffeurs had to endure was the smell of wet fur coats.

A conscientious chauffeur paid as much attention to the underneath of the mudguards as to the top.

Given time, the chauffeur could erect screen, hood and windows for the passengers, but in frosty weather there was nothing to prevent icicles forming on his fine moustache.

Indian princes employed regiments of chauffeurs for their fleets of cars.

Evidently this employer shared with his chauffeur not only his enthusiasm for motoring but also his food. It was more usual for the chauffeur to enjoy his picnic at a discreet distance.

Chauffeurs were expected to wash the cars before putting them away. So that they could be cleaned in all weathers the concrete or cobbled 'wash' was covered with a glass roof.

Clambering up to load luggage on the roof rack was hazardous enough. To handle this top-heavy vehicle, particularly on tramlines or wet roads, called for much skill on the chauffeur's part if disaster was to be avoided.

To the driver of a pedal car the chauffeur of a Rolls-Royce was a godlike figure to be treated with respect.

British families abroad usually employed local chauffeurs.

Peter Robertson had his first taste of it in 1911. His employer had retired the year before, handing over his business interests to his son. Thus freed, he decided to spend the winter in Egypt, travelling by train as far as Marseilles and taking ship there. For the return journey he planned to disembark at Naples and to do a tour of Italy and France on the way home. The party would consist of his wife and himself, a daughter and her fiancé, and two friends. Six people and a chauffeur would obviously mean that the big Isotta Fraschini would be uncomfortably crowded, so he bought a second smaller one. Peter would, of course, drive the big car as usual, but even that man of many parts could not be expected to pilot both.

There was still a general feeling remaining from the early years of the century that French chauffeurs were best, and as half the tour would be in France it seemed sensible to engage one.

Peter planned the route together with the daughter's fiancé, and the little convoy crossed the Channel one gusty day in March, 1911. They covered some two hundred and fifty miles each day, starting at nine and continuing for a couple of hours after dinner, reaching the hotel scheduled for the night stop at ten-thirty or eleven. The weather was bad and the great clumsy capecart hoods gave little protection. On several occasions the party stopped at wayside inns to dry their clothes.

With almost no traffic and with the strong beams from the huge acetylene headlights, driving at night was pleasant when the weather was fine, but one evening near Dijon it started to snow and the flakes froze as they fell. Peter deemed it safer to call it a day. All the same, they reached Cannes on schedule and spent a day in a garage there servicing the cars. The French chauffeur, Georges, proved something of a disappointment. He was an indifferent driver and had but scanty mechanical knowledge. Furthermore, his Parisian French was not easily understood by the natives of Central France and in the Midi he was quite incomprehensible.

After leaving Cannes they had to make a detour because the coast road was blocked by a landslide. There were no *Déviation* signs and they soon got lost in the *Alpes Maritimes*. The big car – designated 100/120-horsepower – was quite at home in the mountains, but the new 35/45-horsepower one, which was nearly as big, was grossly under-powered and, grinding along in first gear, it soon began to boil. The rough tracks caused three punctures; a stone thrown up by the leading car shattered the windscreen of the following one; and altogether the travellers had a bad day.

Things improved once they were in Italy, except that Georges gave up all attempts to make anybody understand him. Peter, on the other hand, got along very well without a word of any tongue except his native Highland Scottish. He managed to get exactly what he wanted by sheer force of personality alone. The roads had not improved since Lionel de Rothschild's adventure with the carter, but these later travellers had a very different outcome to a somewhat similar experience on the Bracco Pass. A donkey pulling a light cart took fright at the sight of the cars and bolted. Fortunately it chose to gallop near the cliff side of the road, not the precipice, and it came to a halt when a wheel shattered against the rock. But instead of coming at them with a knife the carter approached the travellers with a smile and outstretched hand. The hand, of course, was palm upwards and Peter was very quickly able to buy his way out of the incident.

Except for a few punctures, no more troubles arose on the outward journey and they reached Naples exactly as planned, with ample time to get the cars thoroughly cleaned before the liner was due from Port Said.

Although Peter's employer had handed over his business to his son, he could not resist meddling from afar, and he instructed Peter to drive the big car with four passengers direct to Rome as fast as possible for he expected mail to be awaiting him at the hotel. The rest of the party followed at a more leisurely pace and by a circuitous route in the smaller Isotta.

On arrival in Rome, Peter found himself acting as a sort of courier-cum-secretary, taking messages from his employer's suite to the hall-porter or to the restaurant, as well as delivering letters to the British Embassy and to various friends of the employer who were living or staying in Rome.

One day Peter noticed that his employer's usually jovial countenance was overcast with a frown of annoyance, and he heard him growl, 'Bloody impertinence,' as he read one of the reports from his office. He then took a telegraph form and sat holding it for a minute or two, deep in thought, Then his brow cleared and he scribbled a message. 'Take this down to the hall-porter, Peter, and ask him to send it off without delay,' he said with a smile.

Peter read the telegram on the way down in the lift. Its message was simple.

'Tell the beggar to go to Hull.'

But not all telegrams were outgoing. The smaller car was thirty or forty miles south of Rome when the gear-lever snapped. The break was low down, just under the 'gate', and it rendered the car undrivable. The only thing to do was to telegraph for help, which the passengers duly did. Addressed to the owner at his hotel in Rome, the message read, 'Lever broken. Need towing. Please send Peter.' At least, that was how it was written. By the time it arrived the first two sentences had been transliterated by the Italian telegraphist so that it read, 'Liver broken. Need loving. Please send Peter.'

The fiancé of the girl who had written it remarked that in its final form he would have preferred it without the last sentence. As a result the new Isotta Fraschini, that proud Italian marque, entered the Eternal City on the end of a tow-rope.

But the hazards and drawbacks of motoring on the Continent were far outweighed by the advantages. The tourists could go where they liked, stop for as long as they liked and, if they still continued the habit of spending the greater part of their holiday at one base, they could make lengthy expeditions from it.

As far as chauffeurs were concerned, they were visiting places which otherwise they would have had no possible hope of seeing except in time of war. They were enthusiastic about their new experiences and they loved talking about them. In one London mews every chauffeur had been abroad one summer and they would congregate endlessly to discuss their adventures – the level crossing without any gates, the fast run from Avignon to Paris, the snowstorm in the Jura, and the time the brakes failed in the Alps (a common experience, this one). There were still a few horses stabled in the mews, and behind a few of the double doors were still housed carriages, with the coachmen occupying the flats above. One coachman grew heartily sick of all this talk about Europe. A stuck-up lot, those chauffeurs, he considered, with their boasting about average speeds and highly improbable amorous adventures. He himself had never been farther than Brighton, and then the missus went too. It was time for the daily drive round the park – quite far enough, too, no call to go gadding all over Europe – so he left the chauffeurs at it and went to harness the horses.

As he skilfully guided the carriage through the line of parked cars one of the chauffeurs called out to him, well knowing the answer, 'Where are you going today, George?' The coachman flourished his whip. 'Continental touring!' he replied.

James Emergent

Hostility towards the motor car was slow to die, and even as late as the years immediately before the First World War, there were protagonists of the horse who vowed they would never set foot in one of those devilish contraptions. Only slightly less like King Canute defying the waves was the old gentleman who, after a country house visit, suffered himself to be transported to the railway station in a limousine. To his host and hostess he made no protest, containing himself with difficulty, but on arrival at the station he could bottle it up no longer. Handing the chauffeur a substantial tip he told him, 'Here you are, young man. And if you'd been driving a carriage and pair it would have been twice as much. Good day to you.'

But the die-hards were fighting a rearguard action. Cars had become so much more reliable that in many households they were accepted as being the most sensible way of getting about. Within the larger establishments they replaced several types of horse-drawn transport, and every time a carriage was subtracted a car was added. Even comparatively modest car-owning households would probably end up with three – one for the master of the house, one for his wife, and the third for running errands. Three vehicles were more than one chauffeur could manage, so that, as cars proliferated, so did chauffeurs.

Paradoxically enough, the more chauffeurs there were the less they needed to know, and it became far less usual to send a potential chauffeur to a factory for a course in mechanical knowledge. When, for instance, the wife of Peter Robertson's employer got tired of being driven about in the open Isotta Fraschinis, she bought a Fiat landaulette of her own. Even Peter, himself a highly skilled mechanic, seemed to think that the garden boy, after a couple of mornings spent under instruction in the garage workshop and two afternoons trundling round the empty lanes of rural Perthshire, had become a suitably qualified chauffeur. Certainly his experience of looking after the lawn-mowers made him take kindly to the eternal cleaning of the car. He also soon showed that he possessed a characteristic essential to a good chauffeur – attentiveness to his passengers' welfare. Before setting out for the regular afternoon drive he would study the sky and decide whether the sun was likely to remain out long enough to justify the letting down of the landaulette hood, or whether there was a slight nip in the air, in which case he would fill with hot water the long copper cylinder which fitted into the raccoon-skin foot-warmer. When his employer entered the car he would solicitously tuck the rug round her knees – in spring and autumn a woollen tartan one, in winter one made of mus-quash backed with blue cloth to match the carpet. Always, whatever the weather, he would ensure that the tapered silver vase mounted in its ring on the bulkhead between the rear compartment and the driving seat had fresh flowers in it, scented if possible. His previous employment under the head gardener made it easy for him to obtain the first violets, lilies of the valley, wallflowers or carnations.

Only when all these formalities were satisfactorily completed did the Fiat lumber out of the drive – usually, though not always, narrowly missing the nearside gatepost. He really was an appallingly bad driver, but it did not greatly matter.

Perhaps more attention was paid to driving skill in London where, with a great many horse-drawn vehicles as well as cars, the traffic was heavy. But even there it was taken fairly casually. One applicant for the post of under-chauffeur did not expect to have his driving ability examined, and when he was told to take the limousine to Belgrave Square, then to Fortnum and Mason, and finally back to Grosvenor Square he assumed that it was his knowledge of London which was being tested. However, when the drive was over the head chauffeur, who had been sitting impassively beside him, opened the rear door and showed him a bucket of water, full to within an inch or two of the brim, standing on the floor. 'All right. But if you'd spilt a drop of that water you wouldn't have got the job.'

This was more an example of the tyranny which head chauffeurs were now beginning to exercise, having somebody under them for the first time, than any sign of a demand for higher driving standards. Likely lads were still recruited from the younger members of the staff already employed, and given, at best, a few hours' instruction by the head chauffeur. Sometimes there was a job to do with cars, but not involving driving them. For instance, one garden boy was shown how to attach the Stepney wheel and was taken like a diminutive riding mechanic to perform this task if – as often happened – the lady's car suffered a puncture. These jaunts gave him a taste for motoring and he applied for, and obtained, a job as a car washer. It was one step up the ladder which would lead, when he was old enough, to chauffeurdom.

His employer owned an estate on the edge of Salisbury Plain, and the cars always came in coated in the thick white chalk dust. The head chauffeur was a Scot, stern and dour – *not* Peter Robertson – and he exercised a very harsh discipline. Seventy years later a very old man still remembered crying himself to sleep every night. He also remembered the lesson he had learned, the hard way.

'I was cleaning the Silver Ghost one day and I had washed the wheels and carefully dried the bodywork. The head chauffeur stood looking on in complete silence. Then, when I stepped back feeling at least a little pleased with myself, he took a bucket of water and threw it all over my handiwork. "Now," he said, "Let me see you clean a car properly".'

What the boy did not realize was that if somebody is intent on finding fault they always will. In this case the fuss was over a small streak of chalk on one of the wooden spokes of the 'Artillery' wheels. The boy considered the whole episode to be a grave injustice, but with the passing of the years he came to see that it had taught him a valuable lesson. When he, in his turn, became a head chauffeur he imposed the same high standards – but with the important difference that, remembering his own resentment at what he had considered harsh and unfair treatment, he used methods less draconian.

Looking back on it all, he felt that it had been worthwhile, even though this gradual and prolonged approach march to the actual driving had been wearisome at the time. And he was by no means unique. Many a chauffeur came as it were obliquely to driving, and while they had plenty of opportunity to ride in cars which other people drove they were given no regular driving instruction before being put in charge of a car.

This haphazard, step-by-step indoctrination was the general rule, and it obtained even in royal employment. There was, for instance a chauffeur named Hugh Lucas who was first engaged as a footman. His job was to ride beside the chauffeur who remained seated at the wheel while Lucas nipped out and opened the door.

He was nineteen in 1910, and he joined the Royal Household just after King George v had come to the throne. Almost at once he was involved in the annual migration to Balmoral when everybody packed into the royal train. Although King Edward vii had had his own cars driven to their destinations on the Continent King George preferred his to travel on the train in spite of the journeys being much shorter than those which his father had made. Probably the reason was that the royal train would be making the journey with all its passengers and, as it was going in any case it might just as well take the vehicles. There was quite a fleet of them. The largest were two huge 57-horsepower Daimlers, their limousine bodies painted the distinctive deep maroon. Then there was a green Daimler limousine of 38-horsepower for Queen Mary, a couple of shooting brakes, also Daimlers, and a Leyland van for luggage.

Six months after the death of King Edward, Stamper left the royal service, and for the next quarter of a century the head chauffeur was Oscar Humfrey. He had under him four other chauffeurs, two men to wash the cars, and the footman, Hugh Lucas, who was occasionally allowed to try his hand at driving when there were no passengers. These journeys were seldom longer than round the stableyard, but one day Humfrey and Lucas were returning to Buckingham Palace from some way out in the country. On a deserted stretch of road Humfrey brought the big Daimler to a halt and turned to Lucas. 'Well, here's your chance. Let's see how you can manage this on the road.'

The chauffeur was a kind man, and also imperturbable. His act of committing the King's car to the inexperienced twenty-year-old footman was a carefully calculated risk, and one which was fully justified. Concentrating like mad, the tip of his tongue protruding from his lips, Hugh Lucas engaged first gear and gingerly let in the clutch. The great cumbersome car lumbered off, weaving erratically from side to side. But, with his mentor sitting impassive beside him, the young man soon gained confidence, and apprehension gave way to incredulous delight. Here was he, twenty years old and a footman, sitting up high and proud at the wheel of one of the most powerful cars in the world –and one, moreover, which was the personal property of His Majesty the King Emperor. It was one of those occasions which, like a shaft of sunshine, suddenly illuminate the history of the whole trade of chauffeuring.

Lucas was soon to drive regularly – Queen Mary on shopping expeditions, and the royal brothers, the Prince of Wales (later the Duke of Windsor) and the Duke of York, who was to become King George VI.

At a time when the passenger compartments – as opposed to the front, where the chauffeur and footman sat – were fitted up with all sorts of luxurious knick-knacks. Queen Mary's cars were always puritanically austere. Even the seats were of plain leather rather than the cosier Bedford cord or West-of-England cloth. It was not that she did not care. In fact she took the closest interest in the details of the coachwork. She would make several visits to the coachbuilders, Hooper, when a new car was under construction. She tried out cushions of various thicknesses until she was satisfied that she would be sitting at precisely the right height, not an inch too high or too low, so that her face would be framed fair and square in the window as she inclined her head in gracious acknowledgement of the public's welcome. Unthinkable, of course, that there should be any danger of the toque, so distinctive and worn with such distinction, ever touching the roof. On one visit to Hooper's she suggested an innovation which has since become standard practice. The window frames were of wood, like those of an old-fashioned railway carriage, and an inch and a quarter wide. Queen Mary was concerned that they would obstruct the view, both of and for her, unnecessarily, and had them replaced by metal frames only three-eighths of an inch wide.

This idea of the passengers sitting, all warm and snug, and the chauffeur out in front, exposed to the elements, was curiously slow to change. It was of course a relic of carriage days, when it was obviously sensible for a coachman to sit where he could have full control over his horses. As he could hardly have the horses inside the carriage he was forced to be outside with them, reins in his hand and whip by his side. But it did not seem to occur to anybody for a very long time that it was not absolutely essential for the chauffeur to sit out there battling with the elements.

Perhaps he would have been allowed to come in out of the cold sooner if the difference in comfort between open and closed cars had been greater. But although the early limousines were most luxuriously fitted and equipped they were mounted on chassis whose spring design left much to be desired. Bucketing along over the indifferently surfaced roads they shook, rattled and squeaked. Car-sickness was very common in closed cars, but much less so in open ones. It is significant that before the First World War landaulettes were very popular. This was the name given to coachwork where the roof was fixed from the windscreen as far as the rear edge of the doors to the passenger compartment. From there back was a 'soft top' which could be folded down. Only at very low speeds can this have been tolerable, otherwise the draughts and the exhaust fumes sucked in would have made landaulettes unbearable. But on sunny days at low speeds landaulettes were pleasant, providing a welcome alternative to being cooped up in a limousine with the rattles and squeaks reverberating round the enclosed space. It was not only the fascination of watching the driver at work which made children so eager to ride outside, beside the chauffeur.

On the whole chauffeurs did not complain about driving open-fronted cars, and some of them were glad to be at least partially isolated from their employers. It was rare for the isolation to be complete. Closed cars nearly all had a window which could be let down between passengers and chauffeur. If the wheelbase was short the employer could lean forward to speak, and, if unable to make himself – or perhaps more frequently herself – heard above the din, could catch the chauffeur a clip round the back of the neck with an umbrella. In larger cars the chauffeur was safe from this form of assault because heaving oneself up from the seat and advancing, with head bent to avoid the roof, was a perilous business in a car rolling and swaying from side to side. Rather than go through this manoeuvre to reach the front window most passengers resigned themselves to letting the chauffeur get on with it.

But a really determined backseat driver will always find a way. One ingenious device was a battery of bellpushes in the rear compartment, each labelled with a different instruction – 'Right', 'Left', 'Faster', 'Slower', 'Stop'. When pressed a corresponding message would light up on a panel which had been mounted on the dashboard in front of the chauffeur. The trouble was when two side-roads or drive gates were close together. The passenger had to give the order to turn in time to allow the chauffeur to perform the necessary preliminary braking and gear-changing, but if the order was given too far in advance the chauffeur might take an earlier turn than that intended.

Perhaps the most absurd ritual of command to the driver was that evolved by Kaiser Wilhelm II. An ADC would sit in the back of the car beside him, and it was this ADC who was the first link in the formal chain. The Kaiser would tell him what he wanted, and the ADC would press the appropriate button in the control panel let into the side of the car next to him. This caused a light to come on in the panel set – not in front of the chauffeur, but in front of the passenger seat beside him. This seat was occupied by another ADC, who transmitted the command to the driver.

A simpler, and more satisfactory device was a speaking tube. The better ones had an ivory mouthpiece with a stopper with a silk anchor-rope so that it could hang free without falling to the floor. It would be hung on a hook positioned on the side of the rear compartment on which the owner – or whoever gave the instructions – was in the habit of sitting and would terminate in a metal trumpet mounted close to the chauffeur's right ear. He had to school himself to expect a bellow at any moment and not to jerk the wheel in fright so that the car ended up in the ditch. All the same, an order given through the speaking tube was usually followed by a lurch as the chauffeur took his hand from the wheel and touched his cap in acknowledgement.

One owner, whose chauffeur had until quite recently been his coachman, had been indoctrinated with the sensible rule of 'never speaking to the man at the wheel', so he forebore to ask why the car had slowed down. They were passing a railway bridge at the time, visibility was good, there was no other traffic, and the road was quite wide. There seemed to be no reason why the chauffeur should have dropped speed to a crawl. However, he accelerated again and the owner forgot the incident. He was reminded of it a few months later, though, when exactly the same thing happened at the same spot. They had not passed that way in between and he was curious, so he asked the reason. The chauffeur looked at him blankly. For himself, he said, he could not remember having slowed down.

It was not important, and the owner let the matter drop. Until, that is, the next time they drove past that bridge and once again the chauffeur slowed down. This time the owner was determined to get to the bottom of it. He told the man to stop and then asked him why he always dropped his speed to a crawl when they came to that particular place. The chauffeur looked sheepish.

'I suppose it must be habit, sir,' he said. 'You see, the horses always used to shy at that bridge.'

78

James Emerged

The earliest cars were intended to be driven by their owners. The owner would probably employ a man to look after it, but his function was more that of riding mechanic than of chauffeur. In those very early days cars were used for almost identical purposes on both sides of the Atlantic, but soon the concepts were to diverge. As cars became bigger and more reliable, the European owners took it for granted that they would need the services of a chauffeur. However, in the United States the manufacturers were already seeing the possibilities of the automobile becoming the commonplace that it now is. Consequently, much earlier than their European counterparts, they concentrated on simplicity and reliability, their products making up in ruggedness for what they lacked in refinement.

The consequence was that in America the first thing people did when they thought about getting a car was to decide who in the family would drive it, whereas the first thing a European family would do was to engage a chauffeur. Of course the bigger, grander cars on both sides of the Atlantic were designed to be chauffeur-driven, but the employment of a chauffeur was much more usual in Europe than in the United States. For instance, the American family who decided in 1915 to acquire a car arranged that the eldest daughter, aged twenty-three, should be given a lesson – one was considered enough – by the 'sales lady' who delivered the car. The car was not new, a one-year-old Reo, but the idea of being in control of it so terrified the daughter that she refused even to get into the car, let alone drive it. Regretfully, the mother of the family informed the sales lady that she was unable to take delivery and that the automobile would have to be taken back to its garage.

At this point the thirteen-year-old brother stepped forward. Could he, he pleaded, be allowed to try his hand? After all, he reminded them, he could ride a bicycle, in fact did frequently ride one. As for larger vehicles, he had driven a team of carthorses. And finally, most telling of all, he announced that he knew several makes of car. He was, he might as well tell them, perfectly well aware what all the controls were. Clutch, brake, throttle – and that stick thing in the middle is the gear-shift. To clinch it he ended with the familiar cry: 'Oh, Mom, *please!*'

The mother was doubtful, but her daughter added her own entreaty. Provided she did not have to drive the thing herself she really wanted that car. They had been talking about it for weeks and to send it back now would be too terrible. Finally, the mother reluctantly gave her consent. Her son could go off for an hour with the sales lady to see if by any chance he really could get the hang of the thing. She had hardly finished speaking before he had leapt into the driving seat. The sales lady gave a pull on the starting handle and when the engine was running came and sat beside the boy.

'Foot on the clutch. Press it down. That's right. Now the gearshift. Back, slightly towards you. OK. Now let in the clutch gently. *Gently.* Oh.'

The Reo bounded forward and stalled. The boy tried again. This time all went well. Under the instructions of his calm and patient companion he was soon able to return and announce to his mother that he was ready to prove that he had made no idle boast. He could drive, he assured her, he really could. The remainder of the family clambered aboard and away they went. After a couple of hours of, if not incident-free, at least accident-free driving, they returned home with the boy's appointment as family chauffeur confirmed.

But while he was the envy of his schoolfriends, not all the inhabitants of the town took quite such a tolerant view. One day he was sitting in the Reo waiting for his mother who was shopping in the main street of the little village when the majesty of the law approached in the shape of the Town Marshal. He had, he said, received complaints about a young boy driving a car. Might he, he enquired politely, see the driving licence? Well no, no licence. Age? Thirteen.

The Marshal pondered this information, unsatisfactory as it was. But he was a fair-minded man and he readily agreed that there had been no suggestion of reckless driving. All the same, thirteen was a bit on the young side.

Yes, admitted the boy, you could say that. On the other hand driving a car was really quite easy, was it not? The Marshal, outflanked, was forced to admit that he had never driven himself. Then no doubt his chauffeur would be able to tell him how easy it was. Oh, he had no chauffeur? He did not own a car?

The Marshal began to wish he had never started this conversation. But having begun he must carry on to the end. With a masterly stroke he regained the initiative. He would give the boy a test. If the boy could drive him around the village for half an hour without frightening him he would overlook the irregularities.

The unlikely pair set off, the boy on his best behaviour, the Marshal sitting erect and paying close attention to the way in which the controls were manipulated, though he had not the faintest idea what it was all about. At the end of the half-hour he pronounced himself satisfied. But to his verdict he added, quite literally, a rider. The lad must always have an adult in the car with him. Boys, he fully realized, will be boys, but they have less chance to be so if there is a grown-up about.

The boy accummulated a few more years and many more miles driving the family car, and as soon as he was considered old enough he took a regular job as a chauffeur. This he enjoyed for twenty years or so before going into business on his own account.

American college boys were far less inhibited than their European counterparts when it came to vacation employment. If they had no car of their own they were perfectly happy to drive somebody else's, especially when paid to do so, though many of them drew the line at wearing chauffeur's uniform.

One young man, son of a tycoon, answered an advertisement for chauffeur to a Boston lady who owned a Peerless limousine. His previous experience had been on a steam car and the first time he took his new employer out was also the first time he had driven a petrol-engined car. Its gearbox was a complete mystery to him. Heads turned on Commonwealth Avenue Hill as he attempted to shift from high to second amid horrible screeching and grinding of tormented gear-teeth. His employment very nearly ended then and there, but he managed to talk himself out of it and quickly mastered the unfamiliar controls, remaining as chauffeur until the end of the vacation.

When the United States entered the First World War in 1917 the country experienced the acute shortage of drivers which England had felt three years earlier. This provided golden opportunities for the very young and resulted in some fairly odd customs. In one small town funerals could be conducted only in the late afternoon, for at other times the driver of the hearse was in school. In fact, though, the convenience of the dead was better catered for than the welfare of the living, who could be driven to hospital by ambulance only on school half-holidays.

Soon after the end of the First World War, Lambert Ninteman was working as mechanic in charge of a fleet of trucks belonging to a soft drinks bottling plant in Los Angeles. The owner of the plant, who was semi-retired, also owned a hotel at the foot of the San Bernardino Mountains, some seventy-five miles from the city. It had been turned into a convalescent home for soldiers, and the owner paid periodic visits to inspect his property. He found the journey irksome by taxi so he acquired a car of his own and arranged that Ninteman should drive it in his spare time. The overtime pay was welcome but the real incentive was the opportunity to drive the car – one of the great American classics: a 'Big Six' Studebaker. It was capable of speeds of over seventy miles per hour, and both of them loved it. 'Open up the windshield and leave the wind blow through your hair,' the old owner instructed his young chauffeur.

Another young man who owed his start as a chauffeur to the First World War was Douglas Crapser. He had taken a business course and was working in his father's shop when the United States entered the war. In his spare time he helped out at the local garage, and when the chauffeur of one of the customers left to join the Army Douglas took his place. When the original chauffeur returned from the war Douglas went back to the garage and gradually earned the reputation of being a highly skilled mechanic. He had been born on the Vanderbilt estate, and one day Cornelius Vanderbilt called at the garage and asked to see him. When they had shaken hands Vanderbilt said, 'Douglas, would you like to come and work for me?'

'Well,' replied Douglas, 'that depends on the money situation.'

Clearly the thirty-five dollars a week which was offered was considered satisfactory and Douglas became the Vanderbilt chauffeur in

1920, remaining in the job until the death of his employer eighteen years later.

The payment was probably a little higher than the norm, but not greatly, a hundred and fifty dollars a month being quite usual.

In the early 1920s cars still needed a lot of maintenance and many Americans employed chauffeur-mechanics on a part-time basis, largely to take care of the servicing. Even for full-time chauffeurs it was customary to set aside the first hour of the day for the routine maintenance which would be bound to include some greasing – a Pierce Arrow had grease-cups which needed a quarter turn every day.

A very specific schedule of duties was presented to one chauffeur who took up his appointment in 1920, after war service. The employer, a retired shipbuilder, amplified the written instructions. 'First and foremost', began the old autocrat, 'I run this house like the captain of a ship. The clock in the entrance hall will be our time centre. Synchronize your watch with it daily. Report for work at eight a.m. from Monday to Saturday unless you are told otherwise. The car is to be dust-free, tank full, and in perfect running order. It is to be at the front door at nine a.m. except on wet days. Nine o'clock – not five minutes before or five minutes after.'

The chauffeur was warned to study the instruction manual and to abide by its very letter. Evidently he managed to keep everything shipshape because, in spite of the exacting requirements, he regarded this employment as a very good job and only left it when he took to civil engineering.

In the 1920s motor cars were becoming quite common in the United States, but were still something of a rarity in South America. There was great excitement at one *estancia* when the owner bought a car, and much speculation as to which of the cowboys would be chosen to drive it. Even allowing for the benefit of hindsight, it seems strange that the honour should have fallen to one who was already, long before the car arrived to confirm its appropriateness, known as 'Simple Sam'.

Soon after the car came, some neighbours paid a visit to the *estancia*, and their daughter went to see how Sam was getting on with his new charge. She found him in a strange state. At one moment he was puffing out his chest and strutting round the stableyard, supremely proud of his important new status. The next he would be apprehensively glancing over his shoulder.

The girl begged to be shown the new car and, after only the slightest hesitation, Sam led her towards the garage. As he opened the doors he crossed himself and muttered something under his breath. Then he squared his shoulders and walked up to the car. The next ten minutes were spent inspecting the dashboard, while Sam proudly explained what everything was. The girl was made to sit in each seat in turn, wiggle the gear-lever, place her hands on the steering-wheel, and in fact do everything short of starting the car and driving it out of the garage.

When she had sucked dry that particular orange she tried to think of something else. Sam was clearly so proud of the car that it would have been heartless to display less interest. The only thing she could think of to ask was the position of the spare wheel, knowing full well that it was mounted on the back. The question had a curious effect on Sam. The smile left his face, his shoulders drooped, and a hunted look came into his eyes. Dumbly he led her round to the back of the car.

The spring had gone out of his step, and he looked so dejected that the girl felt justified in asking whether there was anything on his mind. He hastened to assure her that there was nothing, absolutely nothing. But it was so apparent that something was wrong that she pressed him. Finally he admitted that there was something which worried him, and worried him very much. Yes, it was about the car. He did not like to ask the *senõr*, who had so kindly bestowed this great honour on him, and he did not like to ask his fellow peons, in case they laughed at him – he had had quite enough of their chaff in the past. But if the *señorita* would be so kind as to explain something to him. . . .

Like many of the first models to have four-wheel brakes this car had an early form of stoplight in which, when the brakes were applied, the word 'STOP' was illuminated. Sam had noticed this the very first day the car had arrived and the light had come on when the man from the garage was turning it round in the stableyard. Although Sam did not actually say so, it was obvious that he thought this red light with its mysterious hieroglyphics had something to do with the Evil Eye. He was haunted by the fear that it might suddenly appear when he was driving along and, of course, from his seat he would not be able to see it. No doubt it was some sort of omen or warning which he would ignore at his peril.

The girl gravely explained that Sam had cleverly made the correct deduction. The light was indeed a warning, just as he had thought. But its message was directed at following drivers, not at Sam himself. It was simply an indication that the splendid car which Sam had been selected to drive, from all the peons on the *estancia*, had awe-inspiringly powerful brakes. Those strange cabalistic signs were letters, and they spelled the English word 'Stop'. When she translated the word he gave a great shout of relief. He rolled it round his tongue. 'Stop. Stop. Stop.'

Next day the smile was back on his face, the spring in his step. 'STOP' no longer held any terrors for him. In fact it was a nice word, unusual and yet easy to remember. Just the sort of name he had been looking for to call his new dog.

Sadly, though, Sam's state of euphoria did not last. He had been almost born in the saddle, and his cow-pony, slightly more intelligent than himself, could get on with the job while Sam happily day-dreamed on its back. But with the car, this 'beautiful new beast' there could be no day-dreaming. It called for more concentration than Sam was able to give. He strove manfully to master it, but it was no good. The effort was killing him, he could bear it no longer.

He went to see the *señor* and confessed his failure. While he greatly appreciated the high trust which had been shown in him, and would always be grateful to the *señor* for singling him out from all the rest, the time had come to admit that he was not worthy of this great honour. He begged to be allowed to 'hang up his gloves and rebuckle his spurs'.

Solemnly the *señor* granted his request, and a great weight slipped from Simple Sam's shoulders. Happily he strode off to take down his saddle, the dog Stop trotting at his heels.

12

Fall in, James

For England the age of leisured luxury, born of Victorian prosperity and nurtured through Edwardian affluence, was at its peak when the twentieth century entered its second decade. The golden, gem-encrusted cornucopia shattered abruptly on 4 August 1914.

War-fever gripped the country. It would be over by Christmas, they said, so 'let's get at it before it's too late' became the cry. Off to the war went the able-bodied men – employers and chauffeurs alike. Patriotism was a word without ambivalence then.

This was the first war in which motor transport played a part. And, just as the taxi-drivers of Paris contributed so greatly to the victory – or at least warding off immediate defeat – by ferrying French troops to the Battle of the Marne, so England had a corps of trained and disciplined drivers and experienced mechanics ready to supply, in the words which Napoleon had used a century earlier, the stomach on which the army marched.

It was a sad come-down from the glistening limousines, disting-uished Daimlers and resplendent Rolls-Royces, to the dull dun-coloured lorries of the Army Service Corps. But the chauffeurs made it. Not without vociferous complaint, certainly, but with soldiers the time to worry is when they cease to complain.

There was, of course, the usual muddle and anomalies inseparable from the sudden expansion of armed services. Hugh Lucas, for instance, the royal footman, spent his first week in the Army answering questions – the same questions – over and over again. The answers established, beyond doubt, his date of birth and religion, but nobody ever asked him if he could drive. Somebody, however, must have assumed that he could, because at the end of the week he was put in charge of a Daimler lorry and told to drive it, in convoy with twenty others, from London to Bulford Camp on Salisbury Plain.

A great many chauffeurs were given jobs driving lorries, and all their skill was needed to keep the convoys moving in France. They would load up at the railhead and set off for the forward dumps, moving in batches of twenty-five or thirty, maintaining a distance of twenty-five yards between vehicles. Distance-keeping was the most difficult part, for if they got too close together there was the risk of having the whole convoy destroyed by shellfire, and if they got too far apart they would lose sight of the lorry in front and quite probably take a wrong turning. In war the first wrong turning a man takes is usually the last turning he ever takes. Because of the long range of the enemy guns all movement had to take place at night, with at most very heavily screened lights and generally with none at all.

While chauffeurs tended to gravitate towards the ASC (it did not become Royal Army Service Corps until 1917), there was scarcely any branch of the services or any theatre of war in which former chauffeurs did not play a part. Perhaps the preponderance was, after the ASC in other corps such as Royal Artillery or Royal Engineers where mechanical knowledge came in useful. Staff officers were naturally quick to seize upon ex-chauffeurs as drivers. This was more agreeable than driving great heavy solid-tyred lorries, but driving any unarmoured vehicle under shellfire was not an experience which many men deliberately chose. From the point of view of protection, as well as of driving, the most desirable vehicles were the Rolls-Royce armoured cars which were used in the Middle Eastern theatre, and not a few chauffeurs, finding themselves at the familiar controls of the Silver Ghost, experienced a wave of nostalgia for the smooth panels which they had polished with such pride and care. Though when the bullets were flying they were glad of the rough slabs of armour-plate.

Not all chauffeurs sought driving jobs. One, who had been a groom before becoming a chauffeur, returned to his first love and enlisted in the Royal Horse Artillery as a driver, being Mentioned in Despatches for bringing his gun out of the line under heavy fire. Another chauffeur found that the trips which he had made to the Continent before the war provided him with what he regarded as a 'cushy' job – that of interpreter, for which he was well qualified, having taken the trouble to learn to speak French fluently while his employer was wintering in Monte Carlo.

But it was as drivers that chauffeurs were mostly employed. With so few cars, compared with later years, driving was by no means a common accomplishment and men who were proficient were eagerly snapped up. Manning the vehicles of the first mechanized army was very difficult, and several survivors remember obtaining a licence at the age of fifteen without being questioned too closely.

The Royal Tanks Corps (later Royal Tank Regiment) was desperately short of the sort of highly skilled and courageous mechanics who could repair under fire the great ungainly tracks, pinning together the hunks of metal so that the monstrous vehicle could trundle on its way. Chauffeurs were worth their weight in gold to the Tank Corps, but even they had to be trained to adapt themselves to a vehicle which was steered with a couple of levers instead of a wheel. One, E. W. Hayward, started as a lad cleaning cars, working up to second chauffeur, then head chauffeur. In 1917 he was driving a tank which came into view of a six-gun enemy artillery battery. 'But,' recalled the eighty-five-year-old Hayward, 'they missed me all the way.' He won the Distinguished Conduct Medal ('other ranks' equivalent of the Distinguished Service Order) and the Military Medal (corresponding to the Military Cross), was eventually commissioned and retired as a Captain in the Royal Tank Regiment.

But it was not only in the fighting services that chauffeurs distinguished themselves, one of whom was George Flack. He was twenty-eight when the war started and immediately tried to volunteer. He was disappointed to find himself rejected on medical grounds, but he was still determined not to be left out. He had recently spent six months with an employer in the South of France, and the country, therefore, held no terrors for him. Off he went, entirely under his own steam, and on arrival in France he joined the French Red Cross, as an ambulance driver. For bravery at Verdun he was awarded the highest category of the *Croix de Guerre*, a decoration which is never lightly given to French citizens, let alone foreigners.

This particularly valiant man was often given little presents by men whose lives he saved, nothing of any intrinsic value, but cherished as expressions of gratitude. Soldiers themselves, of course, received presents from home and many ex-chauffeurs were kept supplied with cigarettes and chocolate by their erstwhile employers. King George and Queen Mary had a standard tin which was sent out, but at Christmas 1914 a very special parcel addressed to Driver H. Lucas was delivered to the Officer Commanding 74th Coy ASC from 4th Army Headquarters. He was instructed to deliver it to the addressee personally. The packet contained a specially large bar of chocolate and was accompanied by a card, personally inscribed 'Best wishes for Christmas' and signed 'Mary RI'.

The following February the Prince of Wales visited the company, and while the Prince was in the Officers Mess Lucas chatted to his chauffeur, whom he had known when they were both employed at Buckingham Palace. The chauffeur told him that the Prince had particularly asked him to try to find Lucas and see how he was getting on, and when the Prince emerged and saw the two men talking he came up to Lucas, shook him by the hand, and passed on messages of goodwill from the King and Queen.

Their Majesties were, of course, by no means the only employers to show concern for their ex-servants in the armed forces. Chauffeurs were often comforted by the knowledge that their jobs would be waiting for them when the war was over, and in the meantime their families continued to occupy the accommodation they had. In fact the employers were not greatly inconvenienced by the chauffeurs' absence, for the petrol shortage reduced motoring to a minimum, and only those engaged on essential work, like doctors, still used their cars freely. Where it was necessary to find a replacement, people took what they could get. A typical example is that of the garden boy who was sixteen when his brother, the chauffeur left for the war, and handed over the job to him. The local garage sent a man to show him how to change a wheel and clean the plugs. He was given two driving lessons and then told to get on with it.

Another chauffeur whose employment precluded him from going overseas was driver for Winston Churchill. He was a teetotaller and this gave Churchill confidence that however long he kept the man waiting while he attended meetings and conferences there was no risk that he would be anything but sober and would never take a nip to keep out the cold. When a Zeppelin was shot down in Essex, the chauffeur later reported, Churchill could not resist dashing off to see the fun. Poking about the smouldering wreckage he saw a glove and picked it up.

There was a hand in it.

As the war dragged on and the casualty lists lengthened, it became apparent that life after the war was going to be very different from what it had been before 1914. The sense of security which employees had felt when promised that their jobs would be held open for them began to evaporate. With their employers dead or impoverished, many of them realized that if they themselves survived the war they would have to look elsewhere. Also, with the increasing number of men who had learned to drive while in the armed services, it was clear that the competition for the chauffeuring jobs which remained would be fierce. For the first time chauffeurs were going to find that there were more applicants than jobs available. And those who thought that their previous experience as chauffeurs would give them a head's start over young men whose first jobs had been as drivers in the Army were dismayed to discover that it was not so. A man who had been driving a lorry, an armoured car, or a staff car for three or four years clearly had all the qualifications necessary, and as the employer was probably an ex-officer himself he naturally tended to place more importance on the man's military record than on his history dating back to those distant, dreamlike days before the world lurched into harsh reality.

13

Come Home, James

It was in the two decades between the Wars that chauffeuring enjoyed its heyday. Before 1914 cars were still relatively scarce, and the driving servant was as likely to be a coachman as a chauffeur. In the 1920s carriages were rare indeed, and while the chauffeur flourished the coachman virtually ceased to exist. The owner-driver had not yet become general, so that the greatly increased number of cars called for a greatly increased number of chauffeurs. It is of course true that individual fortunes were, as a rule, considerably less than they had been before the War, but although wealth was more modest it was more evenly spread, and while on the whole staffs of servants were more strictly limited, most of the households which had had servants before the War still employed a few, and many households which had not previously had any now employed one or two. High on the list of indispensible servants came chauffeurs.

Frequently the household duties would be divided between a married couple, with the chauffeur doubling as butler or gardener or both. But whether he was fifty per cent of the staff or simply one amongst twenty or thirty, the chauffeur assumed considerable importance because of his skills. He became the resident engineer, expected to turn his hand to anything mechanical, from winding the clocks to overhauling the electricity generator.

Just as chauffeurs provided the nucleus of motorized transport for the armed services in 1914, so, at the end of the war, did the armed services provide a pool of skilled drivers for civilian employment. Many of these men found their way into the renascent motor industry, and it is to them that the industry owed its ability to expand so rapidly. Therefore, although there was serious unemployment and far more drivers than there had been before the war, there were plenty of jobs for those who preferred chauffeuring to entering industry.

The most popular jobs were those which offered accommodation, for housing was very difficult to find, particularly in London. Before the war most large houses had a coach-house with a flat over it in the mews at the back, but after the war many of these houses were pulled down or converted into flats. Some owners, like Peter Robertson's employers, retained the mews property when they moved into a flat, and so were able to provide living accommodation for the chauffeur and his family in London. In other cases the chauffeur was paid more, to cover the cost of his own accommodation, but this was never considered to be a very satisfactory arrangement. Prices were usually too high for him to live near his employer and this often entailed long journeys by public transport at inconvenient hours.

But even when it was available, the mews flat was never spacious and seldom even well equipped. Some of them had front doors at street level, others were entered through a small door cut in the big folding doors of the coach-house or garage. A narrow staircase led from the side or back of the garage to the rooms, usually four, above. The rooms overlooking the mews had proper windows but those at the back sometimes had only skylights. Normally there was some way of reaching the main house without going outside, either along a passage from the back of the garage or leading directly from the flat upstairs to the same level of the servants' wing.

Many employers maintained establishments, even modest ones, in both London and the country, but the chauffeur was seldom provided with family accommodation in both places. This meant that he was parted from his family a good deal of the time. While he was living in the country Peter Robertson always stayed in the cottage occupied by the second chauffeur, who was based there. When this chauffeur came to London, he had a room in Peter's mews flat. The room contained a relic of a bygone age, dating back to the time when the house and the mews cottage behind it belonged to the same people. This was the 'blow-through', a speaking-tube used for summoning the carriage. At the house end the butler would inflate his lungs and blow into a mouthpiece. At the mews end there was a stopper with a whistle in it, and when the butler blew the shrill note could be heard not merely in the coachman's flat but all over the mews.

By the time Peter occupied the flat, in 1920, the 'blow-through' had been replaced by a telephone, but his predecessor told him that it had been in constant use up until the outbreak of war in 1914, and that the coachman-turned-chauffeur who occupied the flat then had complained bitterly because it made it impossible to use the room for his children to sleep in. Lack of space in the little flats was a problem experienced by many chauffeurs with families, but although by modern standards, the equipment was for the most part fairly primitive, the lack of facilities seems to have been quite acceptable by the standards of the time.

Chauffeurs living in the country seldom had cause to complain about lack of space, naturally enough, although their accommodation was no better equipped than that in London. It might be a cottage standing on its own, a lodge (where the wife would open the gates for her husband to drive through), or a flat or cottage in the stableyard. One chauffeur, then umarried, recalls that he considered himself lucky in 1920 to be provided with a cottage next to the garage, even though he had to cross the yard to the servants' wing of the main house when he wanted a bath. There was a paraffin stove in the cottage, but he always ate with the other servants in the main house. There was no central heating or gas, but he was allowed as much coal as he needed for the open fires. Lighting was by electricity generated by a rather fearsome engine which he started by swinging a massive flywheel, an operation which required a strong arm and a steady nerve. There was a 'battery house' in which large glass accumulators stored an inadequate amount of electricity, which was sparingly used in both house and cottage.

In the 1920s, before the grid system brought mains electricity to country areas, most houses of any size had their own generating plants. And as most houses of any size also had a chauffeur it somewhat naturally fell to him to run and maintain the lighting plant. Some of these old engines had been installed at the beginning of the century and many a chauffeur spent as much time coaxing them to produce a yellowish glow as he did over servicing the car. The older ones usually ran on paraffin, and petrol was used only to start them.

Although for the most part chauffeurs were well, or at least adequately, housed, there were exceptions, and there are tales of cottages so damp that water ran down the walls of the rooms and fires were kept going all through the summer. Perhaps the most primitive of all was the one in Scotland where the chauffeur and his wife and daughter spent

93

the summer of 1919 when 'the family' were at their shooting lodge nearby. The chauffeur's accommodation was in a farmyard in the village. A building had been roughly adapted for habitation, and consisted of one large room and two bedrooms. There was no glass in the windows, which were covered with wire netting. There was no water laid on to the building, and the nearest sanitation was behind the buildings on the far side of the farmyard.

For the rest of the year this chauffeur had a house rented for him, and he regarded the months spent in Scotland as a sort of camping holiday. There is no record of what his wife thought about it.

Large country houses always had accommodation for visiting chauffeurs, either in the servants' wing or the bothy – a long single-storey building specially constructed for menservants. Another arrangement might be a dormitory over the coach-house. At Clumber Park chauffeurs always hoped to arrive early, so that they could secure a bed as far as possible from the great clock which boomed out above the stableyard in general and the end beds of the dormitory in particular. In all 'host' houses chauffeurs of course had meals provided for them in the house, but there was no fixed rule as to where they should sit. They might be accorded a place at the top table or they might be relegated to the lower table in the servants' hall, or even in the kitchen. It all depended on the attitude taken by those stern dictators of protocol, the butler and housekeeper.

In one respect chauffeurs were more welcome than coachmen – they did not smell horsey. To some extent the chauffeur's status was linked to that of his employer: an earl's chauffeur would almost certainly rate a place at the top table, where the dishes were of silver; chauffeurs of lesser titled folk would have to be content with a place at the long table with the china dishes; and as for the chauffeur of a doctor, parson or lawyer, he would be lucky to get his standing up in the scullery. But there were other considerations. If the employer was a good tipper some of his glory would rub off on the chauffeur, although the converse was seldom true. The sins of the employer were not visited on the chauffeur, for whom there was usually sympathy from servants lucky enough to have more generous employers.

Those country-based chauffeurs whose employers had no London residence would occupy staff rooms at the hotels and would have their meals in a special dining-room. They were completely segregated from their employers, and always used a separate entrance and staircase.

Even on a journey this segregation was rigidly observed whenever they stopped at a hotel for a meal, though it is hard to see the logic behind the thinking that after occupying the same vehicle for several hours the employer and the chauffeur must on no account see each other until the time came to resume the journey. Particular pains were taken to avoid the shock which the employer was supposed to experience if he should chance to meet his chauffeur coming into or out of the lavatory.

Chauffeurs who were based in London tended to live a social life which was an echo of their employers'. They would meet each other at the same houses, restaurants, hotels, or theatres, time and time again. Although the hours they were on duty were very long, they were not working all the time. Much of it was spent in sitting around gossiping or playing cards. Gossip was, of course, fascinating, and a chauffeur with knowledge of a good bit of scandal could be sure of a welcome below any stairs. If it was particularly juicy it would earn him a place near to the housekeeper on his next country house visit.

Nor was it only their employers' affairs which were discussed. When for any reason a chauffeur decided to leave a job, he would pass the information to his friends so that anybody who wanted it could apply. Also a chauffeur applying for a job would ask if anybody knew anything about it, so that he arrived forewarned about the idiosyncracies of the interviewer.

There were several attempts to found clubs for chauffeurs, but they were not successful, mainly because the chauffeurs had so little spare time to themselves. Even if the employer was at a theatre the chauffeur could not absolutely rely on not being wanted before the end of the play, so it was never safe to leave the car for long.

One thing on which a chauffeur prided himself was getting near to the exit of wherever his employer happened to be. Quite outstanding importance was attached to this, by employer as well as by employed. A host who could usher his guests straight into the car when they came out of a theatre felt that his chauffeur had done something clever. The guests were impressed, too, so everyone was happy. Chauffeurs would go to great trouble in their jockeying for position, and not a few commissionaires received bribes to keep 'no parking' signs in place until the giver of the bribe drove up. In the chauffeur's expense account such outgoings were disguised as something innocuous, like petrol.

Life was much easier for the chauffeur who had a second chauffeur or footman riding with him, as many did. This man would meet the employer at the door of the theatre, or the restaurant or house where he had been dining, if necessary carrying an umbrella. He would then take the owner straight to the waiting car in which the chauffeur would be sitting with the engine running. It was little touches like this which good chauffeurs planned with care, for their value was out of all proportion to the time and trouble they saved. It gave the employer great satisfaction to be able to say, 'My fellow has his faults, but I can always rely on him being at the right place at the right time.'

After a day at an office it was a relief to a man to find his car waiting outside and not to have to wonder where it had got to. But perhaps it was more important still at the end of an evening out when the passengers were tired and might have a busy day ahead. It was, for instance, a comfort for people in evening dress to know that, whatever the weather might be, a nice cosy limousine was waiting to waft them home, and that they had only to cross the pavement to reach it.

One wonders whether they would have been quite so pleased with the chauffeurs outside one famous London hotel if they had known how they had been occupied a few minutes before. This hotel had a room in the basement where chauffeurs could sit down and where cups of tea were brought to them. Employers knew about this and were glad that the men did not have to wait outside in the cold. But what they did not know was that on the way down to this room the chauffeurs passed a grating through which they could look up at the dancers on the floor above them. Oddly enough, the chauffeurs often spent so long on the way down that their tea got cold.

14

'This Party-Coloured Livery'

William Congreve

A matter which caused at least as much discussion as the question of what the chauffeur should drive was what the chauffeur should wear. Some employers wished to deck their men out in a certain pomp, others preferred quiet unostentation. Some chauffeurs liked to strut about in eye-catching gaudiness, others felt that distinctive dress was a sign of servility. Often the employer's and the chauffeur's ideas would conflict – and who won the battle was by no means a foregone conclusion.

With this completely new category of servant the choice was wide open, but when confronted with unfettered choice most people look round for a precedent. In this case the nearest equivalent to a chauffeur was a coachman. Unfortunately the coachman's dress was wildly unsuitable for a chauffeur. To start with, the coachman's badge of office was a top hat, and even the most optimistic car owner could hardly have expected a top hat to remain in position on the head of a man driving an open car at anything over the speed of a horse. They therefore turned away from the precedent of a coachman and looked round for some other line to follow. It was sea-farers who provided the answer. A hat designed to stay put in a force ten gale would obviously perform as satisfactorily in any storm which the man at the wheel of a car would encounter. And so, within a few years of the coming of the car, all other forms of headgear had been abandoned in favour of the round hat with the peak. Originally the peak was usually covered in shiny patent leather so that the rain would trickle off, and with a chin-strap to match. As saloon cars became more general the chin-strap was used less and less but was, and is, retained simply for the sake of appearance.

97

In the Navy there is, of course, a badge on the front of the hat above the peak, and this type of headgear looks strangely unfinished without it. Today chauffeurs' hats are nearly always sold with a cockade in the front, but sixty years ago a chauffeur would not assume that he was entitled to the cockade unless he had been told that he was. Even the drivers of very grand equipages often wore a discreet car badge instead. The significance of the cockade has gradually disappeared, but originally it denoted that the wearer was a servant of someone who was a holder of office under the Crown. It was particularly important for coachmen and grooms, because it lent them authority when dealing with innkeepers, arranging the stabling of horses, or the changes of horses at stages on a journey.

The cockade started out as a little bunch of ribbons – white under the Stuart kings, black under the Hanoverians – and gradually evolved into a badge like a rosette with a shallow cone in the middle. Today's little plastic cone with a crinkly edge is a far cry from the white ribbons, both in form and in significance.

Another question which had to be settled before the chauffeur's dress could be ordered was whether it should take the form of livery or of uniform. Livery was the dress worn by servants of a certain family, with details which distinguished it from the dress worn by any other family's servants. Uniform was the dress which indicated the type of servant – coachman, gamekeeper, gardener – without identifying the family of the employer.

Livery was sometimes very brightly coloured – at Stoke Edith the footmen wore peach – but more often it was dark, maroon, bottle green, midnight blue or chocolate brown, occasionally with contrasting collar and cuffs and nearly always with the family crest on silver or brass buttons.

The distinction between livery and uniform frequently became blurred when the chauffeur's dress was designed to match the car. It could be that the car had been painted in the family's own livery colours and that the chauffeur, in matching dress, was wearing livery. Or it might just be that they had chosen a colour scheme that they liked and dolled the chauffeur up in keeping with it.

It would be a great mistake to dismiss lightly the distinction between livery and uniform, because it was extremely important to the chauffeur concerned. It determined his position in the hierarchy of the servants' hall. If it was livery he ranked with the footmen and was not entitled to join the 'pugs' procession when the senior servants took (or had taken for them) their puddings to the privacy of the housekeeper's room. If it was uniform then he was automatically acceped as being among the élite, like the butler, whose black tailcoat and striped trousers were regarded as a mark of prestige.

These niceties were taken very seriously and obtained as long as there was a staff in the servants' hall. Even as late as the mid-1970s the wife of a head porter at a London block of flats was heard to boast that he, of all the head porters in the district, was the only one allowed to wear a black coat and striped trousers.

A coachman in full fig might wear thigh boots and a fur cape, with a leather or oilskin apron draped across his knees, but a chauffeur had to be unencumbered. In an open car without any doors to the front, trousers would not have kept out much rain, so very soon a uniform evolved which consisted of dark whipcord breeches and leather leggings. Chauffeurs who cared about their appearance took a special pride in polishing these leggings. Their tunics were military in cut, double-breasted and fastening at the neck. In winter there would be an overcoat, also double-breasted and coming down almost to the ankles. Some chauffeurs wore gauntlets, some wrist-length gloves, but they were nearly always of brown leather, whatever the colour of the uniform, and very occasionally black.

When the mud of winter turned to dust the chauffeur adopted a long cotton coat, usually fairly light with dark collar and cuffs, and a matching cover for his cap. In the late 1920s, however, the fashion for the dustcoat was gradually abandoned, for by this time cars were most often enclosed. (Technically an open-fronted limousine was called a closed car, and when there were doors and windows for the chauffeur's compartment it was known as 'double-enclosed'.)

Leggings remained fashionable long after the necessity for them had disappeared, their retention depending to some extent on the shape of the chauffeur's calves and the interest of the employer's wife. In the United States puttees were an alternative to leggings, but on both sides of the Atlantic the well-dressed chauffeur had exceptionally well-polished boots.

There was a continuing ambivalence about the colour of the uniform. The great majority of chauffeurs wore either blue or grey, both dark, with sometimes a grey summer suit, lighter both in weight and tone. However it was generally considered permissible to have one's chauffeur dressed in a colour if it matched the car. If it was coloured but did not match the car it was thought to be in hopelessly bad taste. Good taste called for it to be inconspicuous and therefore dark. It was, in fact, all bound up with the old dictum that 'a gentleman's carriage is always black'. This fashion died hard, in spite of the fact that royal cars were deep maroon. Wicker covered panels were acceptable, and there was a short vogue for vertical stripes in alternate dark green and black, but by far the greater majority of chauffeur-driven cars were black or, at the most informal, very dark blue.

One poor chauffeur suffered agonies when his employer bought a car with an open body painted bright scarlet. He had to meet his employer at the local station every night, and whenever the train was late the other waiting chauffeurs would gather round and tease him about 'the fire engine'. He was a sensitive man, and he hated it. He thought about leaving the job but, in spite of his sufferings, it was a good job and he gritted his teeth and stayed.

To his enormous relief his employer announced that he had ordered a closed body to be built. The chauffeur anxiously enquired the colour, and almost fainted with relief when told it would be black. When the car returned from the coachbuilder's he drove it proudly into the station yard. Very stately it looked, with its high roof and big plate glass windows. He pulled up beside the little group of chauffeurs standing waiting. He was smiling confidently, as he nodded affably to his acquaintances. There would be no more silly jokes about fire engines now. He stepped down from the high driving seat and one of the chauffeurs greeted him. 'Hullo,' he said. 'I see your guv'nor's changed his fire engine for a hearse.'

Although an unusual car would invite ribald comments from other chauffeurs, if the chauffeur himself were dressed up in outlandish clothes he was treated with nothing but sympathy. The more independently-minded chauffeurs would make a stand if asked to wear something they thought inappropriate. When Douglas Crapser first entered the Van-derbilt service he fought, and won, a battle of wills with Mrs Vanderbilt. She wanted him to wear a distinctive uniform; he wanted an incon-spicuous one. For some reason he thought that with his great height of six feet six inches he would look absurd in puttees. So trousers it was.

Some chauffeurs, such as Lord Esher's Alfie, took an even stronger line, and refused to wear any sort of uniform for normal duties. Alfie did, however, make one concession. For the sake of the family honour he

ABOVE: Royal Daimlers of 1910. The larger (57-hp) one is of the type in which Stamper made his epic drives between London and Marienbad or Biarritz.

ABOVE LEFT: Boots, leggings, breeches and double-breasted tunics worn with 'cheese-cutter' hats formed the standard chauffeur's uniform from the earliest years of the 20th century until well after the First World War.

ABOVE RIGHT: When war broke out in 1914, women drivers volunteered to drive ambulances, though it cannot have been as enjoyable as these cheerful ladies make it seem. Photographed at Etaples in June 1917. (Imperial War Museum)

The skills of civilian chauffeurs made invaluable contributions to the Army Service Corps (later RASC).

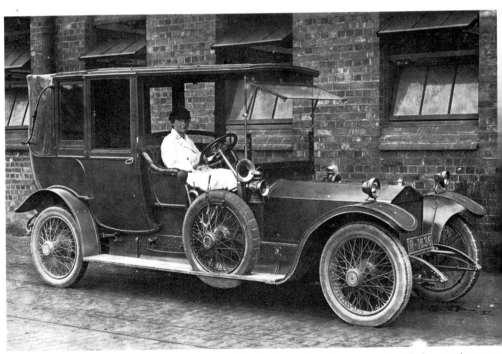

With men away at the war, Chauffeuses often took their places, though not many handled cars as heavy as this pre-war Rolls-Royce shown with Mrs Goring in the driving seat.

Winston Churchill, Minister of State for War, being driven by Bert Lewis in 1919 when he was in Cologne to make emergency arrangements for the military occupation of Germany if the Germans failed to sign the Peace Treaty. In spite of the shape of the moustache, it is unlikely that the figure beside Bert Lewis was Adolf Hitler.

Pola Negri, like many filmstars, liked to be photographed with an impressive car. Her chauffeur's uniform is less formal than those worn by English chauffeurs in the 1920s. (Kobal Collection)

ABOVE LEFT: Thomas Sumner photographed in the early 1920s, wearing the livery of Colonel Proby of Elton Hall near Peterborough. The black uniform has a pale blue collar.

ABOVE RIGHT: Annie Philbey, a chauffeur's daughter, helping her aunt to wash a Wolseley in the mid-1920s. After doing odd jobs and cleaning cars during the war she became second chauffeur and secretary to her employer in Oxfordshire.

BELOW: The Grand Duke Michael of Russia beside his 1914 Silver Ghost Rolls-Royce. He was Czar for one day. Next to him is his chauffeur, who kept his job for longer.

Chauffeurs under instruction. A 1924 20-hp car belonging to the Rolls-Royce School. (John Fasal)

Long delays at frontier posts were accepted as normal, but were found more irksome by passengers than by chauffeurs, who were accustomed to hanging about.

Whispering Chorus was one of the earlier films to use a chauffeur-driven limousine to provide a background of glamour. (Kobal Collection)

Douglas Crapser pictured with the Minerva which he persuaded his Vanderbilt employer to exchange for a Cadillac. (D. Crapser)

It was customary for chauffeurs to touch their hats but not remove them. Only chauffeurs to Royalty uncovered. Queen Mary stepping out of one of her high Daimlers to attend the Armistice Day service of 1923. (Radio Times Hulton Picture Library)

Chauffeurs, as well as footmen and keepers, doubled up as loaders. Photograph, taken at Lord Masserene's shoot in 1929, reproduced by courtesy of Mrs Mercer.

Chauffeur. "I REGRET THE CAR WILL NOT BE AVAILABLE THIS AFTERNOON, MY LADY."
Mistress. "WHY? WHAT'S THE MATTER?"
Chauffeur. "YESTERDAY WAS ONE OF HIS LORDSHIP'S DAYS WITH THE CARBURETTOR, MY LADY."

A chauffeur's attitude towards amateur mechanics ranged from condescension to contempt. A *Punch* cartoon of 1932.

Buster Keaton in *The Navigator* (1924) was the first to use the joke, since well worn, of telling the chauffeur to drive to an address which turns out to be across the street. (Kobal Collection)

consented to dress up once a year when Lord Esher went grouse shooting with the King at Balmoral. But Alfie was not the only problem. The car itself, which was a Metallurgique with a flapping canvas hood, was also considered too informal for these special occasions. Fortunately there was an alternative. Lord Esher also owned a 1918 Daimler limousine, a majestic vehicle which was entirely suitable for creaking its way along Deeside en route for the royal residence. It cannot, though, have been judged to be suitable for much else, because when Lord Esher died in 1930 it had still only covered less than six thousand miles.

There were no such opportunities for coercing into uniform one Bundy, the chauffeur-gardener, factotum and right-hand-man of a lady living in Dorset. A man of immense resource he, like his employer, had a personality larger than life. (Her late husband was once sitting in the hall, taking a breather from one of her parties, when a guest came up and remarked on the wife's boundless energy. Her husband nodded in agreement. 'Yes,' he said. 'Before now I have been sitting in this chair – this very chair – and seen my wife come in through both those doors simultaneously.) She was always trying to persuade Bundy to smarten himself up, and he always withstood her.

One hot day he had been mowing the lawn and was looking more like a tramp than usual as he plodded past the drawing-room window. His employer was giving a tea-party and, happening to see Bundy, she went to the window waving a silver jug.

'Oh, Bundy, get me some hot water would you?' Bundy gave her a baleful glance and trudged off. When he returned she took the jug and said, 'Oh thank you so much.' Then she paused, and added, 'Really Bundy, I do think it's time we got you a uniform.'

Bundy glared at her. 'Yes it is, my lady. A cap and hapron.' He stalked away.

On one occasion he drove her to the station and carried her suitcase on to the platform. She told him not to wait for the train. There was plenty, she was sure, that he might better be doing at home. As he left she noticed an old friend farther down the platform and darted off for a chat. When she went to retrieve her suitcase it had gone.

Weeks later Bundy was at the station and he noticed a taxi with a puncture. The driver was lifting the spare wheel out of the boot and when Bundy went to help he noticed that in the boot there were some familiar clothes. The police were told, the taxi-driver's house was searched and the missing case and its contents discovered.

The employer's daughter congratulated Bundy on his detective work. 'How clever of you to know they were my mother's clothes.'

Bundy looked at her. 'Simple, miss. Nobody except her ladyship would wear stays done up with string.'

But fashions were changing, and the dress of people more sartorially aware than Bundy and his employer were changing with them. By about 1930 it was unusual to see a chauffeur wearing leggings, and even the boots had, for the most part, given way to shoes. Overcoats became shorter, and jackets were cut more like lounge suits and no longer did up to the neck. White shirts with stiff collars and black ties were the normal wear.

In the United States some chauffeurs wore bow ties, but these were very rare in England. There was, however, one man who wore with his chauffeur's cap not merely a bow tie but a jacket with silk facings. He was a keen owner-driver, and possessed a rather splendid Jensen coupé. When the breathalyser was first introduced he got hold of the wrong end of the stick and was under the impression that the police were likely to pounce at any moment, and not merely when they had grounds for suspecting that the driver had drunk too much or had been involved in an accident. Furthermore, he was convinced that a small glass of wine would send him far over the limit. Dining out became a nightmare for him.

However it was not long before he hit upon a solution which, to his mind, solved the problem completely. He had a touching faith in the inviolability of professional drivers. The police, he imagined, would never have the temerity to stop a chauffeur driving impeccably about his business. Accordingly he bought a chauffeur's cap, which he would don when entering his car after a dinner party. Bundling his wife into the back he would drive home, wearing his dinner jacket and chauffeur's cap, secure in his conviction that the cap was a sort of talisman which would protect him against summary arrest. He may be right. He has never been stopped yet.

A nice example of how a smart chauffeur's uniform is appreciated is contained in a letter written to the authors by a 74-year-old pensioner. She describes how she alighted from a train and was approached by a chauffeur who asked her if she was Lady Pamela——. When she said she was not, he explained that he had been sent to meet her ladyship but that he had not previously seen her. 'He had extremely nice manners,' the letter continues, 'and said he was sorry. I thought, you're not nearly as sorry as I am at *not* being the lady in question and being met at the station by such a handsome gentleman plus a car, whether he was a chauffeur or otherwise.'

15

'The Trivial Round, the Common Task'

John Keble

There was a great difference between the way of life of a chauffeur in the country and one in London, but if the employer took part in the social round the chauffeur experienced both, moving from the town house to Cowes for the yachting, to Scotland for the grouse shooting, back to London for the 'Little Season' and then to the country for the hunting, the partridge and pheasant shooting or whatever sporting activity the employer enjoyed. If he was a fisherman he might spend a weekend or two in Hampshire where the Test and the Itchen were then, as now, famous trout rivers, or in Scotland for salmon in the Tay, Spey or Deveron, or perhaps on the Wye in Herefordshire. Slightly less fashionable in the 1920s, but still fairly popular and getting more so, was Continental travel.

None of this, of course, was an absolutely standard pattern, and many business or professional employers never left their own homes except for a short holiday. Their chauffeurs had a much more regular pattern of life and tended to become more integrated with the nearest village or town, playing cricket for the local team, singing in the church choir, or following some hobby or pastime which appealed to them.

If the employer lived in London there was generally a daily routine. Leave for the office at the same time every morning, report to the employer's wife and take her shopping or perhaps out to lunch. There might be another outing of some sort in the afternoon, timed to finish early enough to allow the chauffeur to collect the employer from his office.

Chauffeurs shrewdly assessed the likelihood of evening work, but it was not always predictable. The employer and his wife might be past the age of gadding about and prefer a quiet evening at home, leaving the chauffeur to his own devices. On the other hand there might be daughters who spent several long evenings at nightclubs each week. A chauffeur who discovered that his prospective employer was child-less might look forward to an easy time with an elderly gentleman, only to discover that he owned stalls in Covent Garden and wanted to visit them all too often, leaving home at three o'clock in the morning.

Probably the chauffeurs who worked hardest of all were those employed by doctors. Likely to be called out at short notice at any hour in the twenty-four, they had to fit in the maintenance as best they could and, as the cars were used so much and their reliability was so important, the maintenance could not be skimped.

But at least doctors' chauffeurs spent their whole time with the cars. Jobs which entailed less driving usually meant that the chauffeur was expected to occupy his time with work for which he was often not trained, did not like, and for which he had no aptitude. He might find himself feeding the chickens, digging the garden, rolling the drive, stoking the boiler or even milking the cows. While some enjoyed mixing chauffeuring with other activities – like the man whose mechanical knowledge was found to be minimal but who was highly esteemed by his employer because he was a genius at training spaniels – others resented being asked to dilute the mainstream of their experience with other activities. The ultimate humiliation was when other chauffeurs began to refer to them as 'drivers'.

London chauffeurs scored heavily in this respect. With no chickens or lawns to bother about, the most ex-curricula duties they were asked to perform were tasks like cleaning the inside of windows or helping the indoor staff to dismantle and wash chandeliers. In fact they were usually kept too busy with the cars to have time for anything else. It is probably fair to say that the better the chauffeur was, the more fun he got out of his job, however busy it kept him. Those who were constantly at the wheel had cleaners to help them, and even in London many establishments maintained more than one car, and the grander ones might have up to half a dozen chauffeurs, all fully employed. With the continual round of entertaining, chauffeurs were often called upon to fetch guests or to take them home, tasks which they enjoyed because they nearly always received a tip.

Tips of another kind also added to many chauffeurs' incomes, and jobs with racehorse owners were eagerly competed for. Looking back in his eightieth year, F. R. Ashment remembered how pleased he was to land, in 1927 the job of chauffeur to Sir William Bass who was a Steward of the Jockey Club. The only snag was that he was paid monthly, and if he backed losers in the first two weeks he found the second fortnight rather heavy going. 'We were racing,' he said, 'six days a week.'

For a man who was keen on racing this was an absolutely ideal position. There would be the Guineas meeting at Newmarket, then up to Aintree for the Grand National and the opening of the Flat season at Lincoln. In May the London 'Season' started, with its non-stop round of dinner parties and balls. Sir William always attended the Derby Dinner at Buckingham Palace. These dinners did not involve the chauffeurs in any problems, but it was a different matter when it came to Levees and Presentations at Court, for then there were so many people that the Mall was lined with cars from end to end, all inching slowly forward with the chauffeurs wondering whether the clutch would start to slip or the radiator to boil. There was also the personal problem: there was no hope of getting to a lavatory. The wise ones restricted themselves to a single cup of tea in the morning of the great day.

For functions at Buckingham Palace it was essential to have a footman who could jump down and open doors, so that each car spent only the minimum amount of time setting down and picking up its passengers. Families who did not employ a footman could usually borrow a second chauffeur, either by applying to his employer or by asking their own chauffeur to get one of his colleagues to stand in for the occasion – a useful source of extra money for chauffeurs who were not themselves driving to the Palace.

Some employers preserved a dignified silence, but most of them were eager to tell their chauffeurs all about it on the way home and only too glad to be asked, 'Did you enjoy it, madam?' Sir William Bass, on one occasion, clearly did not because he had been looking forward to the traditional turtle soup and that year there had not been any.

Royal Ascot, for which those not fortunate enough to own houses in the immediate neighbourhood would rent them at enormous prices in order to entertain their friends, and the Aldershot Tattoo, were landmarks in the Season which closed with Goodwood. In 1928 the King and Queen stayed with Sir William Bass near Petworth, and that week marked one of the highspots of Ashment's life. For the drive across the rolling Sussex countryside to Goodwood the royal chauffeur, Humfrey, issued Ashment with a crown to fix above the windscreen.

'It was,' said Ashment 'dream motoring. I drove the car immediately following the royal car, and my orders were to keep seventy yards' distance. The police cleared the way for us and I remember how proud I felt to be driving in the royal procession.' He came down to earth again on the Friday when the time came to return the crown to Humfrey and 'to drive back to London with the common herd'.

After the heady experience of Glorious Goodwood it was something of an anti-climax to drive north to Lowther Castle for the grouse shooting with Lord Lonsdale, that colourful peer with the white side-whiskers and the fleet of yellow cars.

It was at Lowther that a young guest was severely put in his place by Lord Lonsdale's chauffeur. He was trailing round on the Sunday morning inspection and came to one of the Rolls-Royces with its bonnet open and the chauffeur standing beside it. Feeling that he ought to say something, the guest uttered the first thought that came into his head. 'What a huge engine! It must use a lot of petrol. Terribly expensive to run.'

The chauffeur looked shocked. Then he made a dismissive gesture. 'To his lordship,' he remarked coldly, 'the cost of petrol is *nothing.*'

After the stay at Lowther, Ashment drove Sir William to Scotland for the deer-stalking, taking in the St Leger at Doncaster on the way. Back to London for the 'Little Season' and then to Sir William's country house in Derbyshire. The winter was spent fox-hunting (Sir William was Master of the Meynell) and this was a fairly easy time for Ashment, until the round of Hunt Balls began. After that it was time for Cheltenham, and so the Flat racing season came round again.

This busy life was a happy one for a single man, but when he got married Ashment obtained a job which allowed him to remain in one place. It was much less glamorous, but it enabled him to set up a home and give continuity and stability to his family.

Inevitably many employers who led a much less social life than a Steward of the Jockey Club were also often away from home, either in Britain or abroad, and usually they took their cars and chauffeurs with them. The chauffeur's families seldom went too – the family which spent the summer in the barn in Scotland was an exception – and the chauffeur's long absences, often at very short notice, had to be regarded as an occupational hazard.

But if there were drawbacks there were advantages too. It was customary for the employers to provide produce from the estate and, at a time when landowners did not have to be as commercial as they are now, they would not sell game but give it to friends and employees. Chauffeurs' families could rely on pheasant, partridge, hare, and in many cases venison, trout, and salmon as well. Often the man was encouraged to shoot pigeons and rabbits for the pot, particularly if he had the sense to keep on the right side of the keeper. Equally important was to be friends with the head gardener; failure to take these precautions would lead to friction between servants, a thing of which all employers had a horror.

In the years between the wars wages remained fairly steady, and a chauffeur considered himself well off with four pounds a week. In addition he had accommodation for himself and his family, food from his employer's garden and estate, heating and lighting. Meanwhile his uniform allowance included shirts, collars and ties as well as shoes or boots and leggings, and of course the cap. When he was away from home his meals were provided. Although he spent most of his time in the company of people a very great deal richer than himself, he was philosophical enough to appreciate that his own prosperity was a microcosm of theirs. If they fell on evil times, so did he. Acceptance of this attitude was implicit in the job, and men who did not accept it did not become chauffeurs.

Although by modern standards these wages sound pitifully low, they were not considered so at the time, and the reason is apparent if one considers the cost of the cars of the period. Even as late as 1939 a 'Pullman Limousine' Phantom III Rolls-Royce was listed at £2,670, a Cadillac 'Fleetwood' limousine at £1,245, and a Daimler limousine £1,550. All these cars had glass partitions between passengers and chauffeur, and occasional seats. Three people could ride comfortably on the back seat, two rather less comfortably on the tip-up seats, one – or two if they were small enough – beside the driver.

In fact it was possible to get a full seven-passenger limousine for under a thousand pounds. The biggest Buick was £925, and while the Straight Eight Daimler limousine cost £1,550 the 6-cylinder 24-horsepower seven-seater could be bought for £875. The mammoth 8-cylinder, 8-litre, 8-speed Hitler/Goering type Mercedes was listed at £3,450, but the 26-horsepower 6-cylinder limousine was only £880 and a Humber £750. Probably one of the cheapest of these big chauffeur-driven limousines was rather a special case. Minerva had gone out of car production several years earlier, but they were still selling off stock, and were quoting £695 for models similar to the one on their stand at the 1938 Motor Show.

Against these prices, £200 a year for a chauffeur looks quite reasonable, particularly as these are only the largest and most opulent models. A great many chauffeurs worked for employers who would not dream of spending so much, and who did not need such a big car. A 30-horsepower Buick saloon cost about £500 and an 18-horsepower Austin a little over £350, both of them roomy saloons carrying five people in considerable comfort. A Ford v8 of similar size cost £280.

Even though the level of chauffeurs' wages was regarded as satisfactory, it was not enough to make provision for retirement. Most employers realized this, and if the chauffeur had been in their service for a long time they did something about it. The amount of the contribution varied enormously. It might be a pension which ranged from generous to token. Sometimes it was a sort of 'grace and favour' residence where the chauffeur was permitted to spend the rest of his life – and his wife to spend the rest of hers if she outlived him – at only a nominal rent, if not entirely rent-free.

The trouble with this arrangement was that the accommodation was usually needed for the new chauffeur, and even the large estates where a few cottages were kept for pensioners soon found that these cottages became occupied and the chauffeur would either have to go on a waiting list until somebody died or find another permanent home. If, however, the employer was a generous one, and the chauffeur had given long and faithful service, he might even buy a house and give it to him.

Chauffeurs who had not been in the service of their last employer for long enough to qualify for his generosity had usually foreseen the position and made previous arrangements, financial or otherwise, to go and live with a son or daughter. Normally, of course, a chauffeur would not voluntarily leave a job when he was approaching retirement age.

One long-service chauffeur to a generous employer did not receive a rent-free house. This was not due to any meanness on the part of the employer, nor to any dislike of his chauffeur, for whom he had a high regard. It was simply that during the twenty-seven years of his employment the chauffeur had become richer and richer. It all started when he was a young man and went to the Argentine to seek his fortune. He found it in the form of a modest win in the State Lottery. He returned to England and invested the money, not in cautious gilt-edged securities, but in a well-run company quoted on the Stock Exchange. Both company and shareholders prospered mightily, and by the time he was ready to give up the chauffeuring job, which he had greatly enjoyed, he was in a position to buy a very nice house for himself. But that was not all. He also bought two cottages from his employer.

Even though he had now diverted some of his capital into property, he still kept in a prominent place on his mantelshelf a photograph of the chairman of the company which had made him rich.

In the slump years of 1929 and 1930 a number of families found that they could no longer afford a chauffeur. With young chauffeurs this did not greatly matter, because there were other chauffeur's jobs to be had, but for the older men the outlook was grim. The employers – or at least those with consciences – did what they could, but in the bleak financial climate it was seldom much. Perhaps an introduction to a prospective employer, perhaps permission to stay on in accommodation if it was not intended to sell up. Those employers whose own financial plight was less than desperate, albeit severely curtailed from what it had been, did in certain cases make a present of a lump sum in lieu of pension. This enabled the chauffeur to set up in business on his own account, though in those days there were few openings in the car hire business, or in the motor trade, and he would be likely to start in something quite different.

The chauffeurs who turned to car hire were generally those who had a legacy from a deceased employer, either in cash or in car. Employers quite often left substantial legacies to their chauffeurs, but these employers were usually widows. Their husbands would leave the chauffeur enough to keep him loyal but not enough to make him independent – in case he should retire there and then, leaving the widow to find a new servant. It was the widow herself who would make the major bequest. Often this was considerable, particularly if the chauffeur had been sympathetic to her in a time of sadness. Many a widow's sons and daughters experienced anxiety over this. If their mother was full of praise for the understanding, kindness and help which she had received from this paragon of a chauffeur, they began to have grave fears that he would scoop the lot.

Mean employers were in the habit of using the promise of a legacy as a weapon. If the chauffeur complained of being overworked, or had some quite reasonable request or complaint, they would tell him that he was in danger of being cut out of the Will. Another ploy was to pay low wages and make up the difference with promises of a lavish legacy. A certain old harridan played this game with her chauffeur, but it cost her much more than the modest increase in wages for which he had asked.

She was the owner of a very old Daimler. It was a good, reliable car, and perfectly adequate for the short journeys which were all she needed it for. But, shortly after the conversation about wages, it developed a mysterious illness. The chauffeur put it down to senility and the owner was finally forced to the agonizing conclusion that she would have to buy a new one. Perhaps something smaller would do? Smaller and not so expensive. Certainly not, said the chauffeur. He would hate her to have the discomfort of any lesser car. Another Daimler it must be.

Groaning with the effort of paying for it, this very rich old woman bought a new Daimler. She thought it was marvellous, but the chauffeur soon began telling her that it was not a patch on the old one. At one stage he rather overdid it and she tried to get the old one back again, but the chauffeur was able to persuade her that it would have been broken up by now.

One day, when she had had the new car for nearly a year, it failed to start outside a shop and she had to go home in a taxi. The chauffeur then replaced the leads which he had previously removed from the plugs, and soon – but not too soon – drove home. In answer to the lady's anxious questions he gave pessimistic replies. It was, he said, quite likely that it would happen again. Oh dear, what was to be done? There was, he considered, nothing for it but to get a new car. And this time perhaps it would be better to try another make, say a Rolls-Royce.

She bought it, but she died a couple of months afterwards and it was the chauffeur who lived to enjoy it.

16

Never Mind the Weather

The greatest difference between motoring in the Golden Age and motoring today is that we do not dress up for it. Bored or frustrated we may be as we bowl along, but our cars are capsules which both insulate and isolate us from the weather. Furthermore, we can plan anything short of a picnic regardless of whether it is likely to rain or not. It may be pleasanter to drive in fine weather, but there is no physical discomfort in travelling in a saloon car on a wet day. And if the weather turns chilly we can always turn up the heater.

Perhaps the three things which contributed most to a chauffeur's well-being are the self-starter, the windscreen wiper and the heater. Self-starters, like four-wheel brakes, made tentative beginnings while King Edward VII was still alive, but neither was by any means common in the early 1920s. In addition, it was some time before the motor industry recovered from the First World War, and many people used cars dating from before 1914.

Windscreen wipers did not come in until the mid-1920s, and then they were worked by hand. Until well after the Second World War there were many makes of car with vacuum-operated wipers which would stop when the car was accelerated, just when they were needed most.

Heaters, and with them de-misters, were known before the Second World War, but were rare. In the 1950s 'optional extras' included heaters, but they were expensive and not very good.

For at least the first half-century of motoring, therefore, it had to be undertaken in varying degrees of discomfort. Rain or snow in the early days necessitated driving with the windscreen open and in wintertime chauffeurs often had icicles on their eyebrows. After long exposure to the elements even the thickest gloves could not keep out the cold, and chauffeurs often suffered the discomfort and inconvenience of chilblains. The icicles melted when they got indoors, but the chilblains did not.

There was also the hazard of the starting handle swinging round and breaking a wrist; some clutches on big cars were so heavy that they caused ruptures; and the seats caused slipped discs and other injuries to the back. Even with self-starters, windscreen wipers and heaters, there was still the probability that the driving seat would be uncomfortable. In order to provide the maximum amount of room in the passenger compartment the front seat was placed too far forward when it was designed to be occupied by a chauffeur. With the glass partition dividing front compartment from rear, the driving seat had to be fixed and the chauffeur had to adjust to fit the seat instead of the seat being adjustable to fit him. A big man was cramped, a little one had to have a cushion. (It is, incidentally, surprising that it cannot have occurred to owners of chauffeur-driven cars that, before the days of independent rear suspension, the seat over the back axle bounced up and down much more than the one positioned more or less midway between the axles and occupied by the chauffeur. This also explains why so many passengers complained that their chauffeur was driving jerkily, when he was of the opinion that his driving was as smooth as cream.)

The surprising thing is that cars were taken out as often as they were. Even the most luxurious limousine was bitterly cold in winter, whereas the chauffeur did at least have the warmth of the engine filtering back to stop his feet from freezing. In summer, of course, his feet got too hot, and coachbuilders compensated for inadequate insulation by having little doors in the sides of the scuttle which could be opened to ventilate the area round the pedals. Studebakers with touring bodies had a device for locking the doors slightly ajar so that the hot air could escape.

But, however formidable were all these deterrents to motoring, there is ample evidence to show that they were either ignored or else challenged and overcome. There was a universal subscription to the doctrine that if you wait for the weather you will never do anything. There are horrific stories of cars being driven in conditions so bad that one would imagine that people would only have been out of doors in the most dire emergency. In fact, it was not necessarily so. Peter Robertson digging a car out of a snowdrift on the way back from a dinner party, a footman with a white scarf hanging down his back walking in front of a car to guide it through the fog after a visit to the opera, were simply considered to be coping with normal hazards. While thinking that they would all have been much wiser to stay at home, one cannot help admiring the heroism.

Aids to driving were slow in coming, and their development lagged behind the pace of the development of cars. Warning signs did not appear at all in England until after the 1904 Act, and signposts seldom pointed to destinations farther than the next small town. There were no white lines until the 1930s, and cat's-eyes came later still. In the early 1920s the Devon County Council made a great leap forward by painting all their roadside fences black and white so that they would be more easily visible in the dark, but otherwise except in towns there was nothing to help the motorist at night. Minor country roads were very narrow, and in fact it was not until the Second World War that they were widened to take the great volume of military traffic building up for the invasion of Europe. There were no by-passes in the early days, and very few until well into the 1930s. Italy under Mussolini pioneered motorways, and his fellow dictator across the Alps, not to be outdone, followed suit. But in Britain there were no motorways until well after the Second World War.

In view of the difficulties one might expect journeys to have been short, but there are plenty of examples of high mileages. The chauffeur to a salesman drove him on a daily round which amounted to thirty-five thousand miles a year, and this was in no large limousine but in a Model T Ford. Even before the First World War a pleasure drive was often eighty or a hundred miles, and distances of two hundred miles would be completed in a day if en route to a distant destination. The long distances were achieved by keeping steadily on, stopping (voluntarily) only for meals or petrol over a span of twelve or fourteen hours. It was only on these long journeys that the chauffeurs broke their rule of cleaning the car before putting it away.

It was not only the big cars, the Napiers, Rolls-Royces, Daimlers, Hispano Suizas, Isotta Fraschinis, Minervas, Excelsiors, Cadillacs, Pierce-Arrows, Packards, Renaults and Delages, which covered long distances in a day. Smaller models of Armstrong Siddeley, Austin, Morris, Clyno, Citroën, Fiat and Ford trundled determinedly along, notching up the score with a chauffeur at the wheel. One busy doctor's idea of relaxation on his day off was to take turns with the chauffeur driving his Bean two hundred miles to see his daughter, and returning after tea.

There was a sort of halcyon period in the late twenties and early thirties when roads had greatly improved but traffic had not yet become heavy enough to cause delays, and a chauffeur driving a fast car could reckon on covering two hundred miles in four hours. But, if he could do that in the Bentley, for shorter trips he would probably find himself cruising at thirty to thirty-five miles an hour in the Austin Heavy Twelve Four. As late as 1932 Fiat were only claiming 52·8 miles per hour for their little 508 – and chauffeurs advised their employers to buy one as a 'shopping car', because it was 'nippy'.

The length of time a car was kept depended very much on the chauffeur. If he was a good mechanic and the car was of high quality, the owner might keep it until its performance was substantially superseded by one of later design. One chauffeur remembers a Fiat which had done fifty thousand miles when he took the job and which went on to do another two hundred thousand in the same ownership. While this must have been exceptional, mileages which even today would be considered quite high were covered by well-maintained cars, most of which gave a modest power output from big, lightly stressed engines. Seventy or eighty thousand was not uncommon, and HRH Prince Henry Duke of Gloucester made a habit of keeping all his cars, not only his Rolls-Royce, for a minimum of a hundred thousand miles.

The Rolls-Royce Silver Ghost set a standard of excellence long before the First World War. The company started a scheme of inspecting annually the cars which they had sold, and rewarding the chauffeurs who had maintained them properly. These payments were made only with the owner's consent, which was almost always given with alacrity. Not only did he not have to pay out himself, but he had received a reassuring vote of confidence in his chauffeur. In 1919 Rolls-Royce opened a school near Derby. It was primarily for chauffeurs, but owners were welcome too, and it soon became much sought after. A certificate from Rolls-Royce was a credential to impress any employer, whether he owned a Rolls-Royce or not, and once a chauffeur had attended the school he was fairly sure of being able to get a good job anywhere.

The school rather backfired on the company in the mid-1920s, when the replacement for the Silver Ghost was being tested. Chauffeurs saw it, and advised their employers to delay buying a new car until this model became available. The result of this industrial espionage was that sales of the Silver Ghost slumped while everybody held back waiting for the New Phantom. Determined never to be caught out this way again, Rolls-Royce moved the school far away from the factory, but did not interrupt its very thorough curriculum which consisted of about seventy per cent classroom instruction and thirty per cent on the road. Nowadays the course is run at the Service Works on the outskirts of London and still covers the same detailed lessons, including correct behaviour to passengers.

It was not until 1929 that the Daimler company opened their school, and then the course lasted only four days as against the fortnight of Rolls-Royce's.

No other make of car approached the Rolls-Royce in reputation, and it was not until the 1930s that any one alternative gained any great popularity. This was true not only in Britain but in Europe, India – especially in India where maharajahs would have fleets of them, mostly driven by Indian chauffeurs – the United States, and, in fact all over the world. There were, of course, exceptions. Some people preferred the rarity value of one of the great Continental or, more rarely, American makes, and Douglas Crapser sternly told Mr Vanderbilt, 'You only buy European cars for the individuality and the prestige.' He pointed out that the Presidents of the United States drove about in Cadillacs, and persuaded his employer to buy a 16-cylinder one which they both loved. But in England the scene was changing. The country had suffered severely from the slump, and although in the early 1930s things were beginning to pick up, a great many fortunes had been trimmed and slimmed. There were, of course, still very rich people who could indulge a taste for exotic cars, but most of those who had been able to buy a Silver Ghost in 1924 without thinking twice about it found that ten years later they were having to look round for something cheaper than a Phantom II.

With high unemployment it was considered unpatriotic to buy foreign cars, but every effort was being made to stimulate trade with other countries within the British Empire, and in Canada was waiting the answer. The McLaughlin factory had been set up there to build Buicks, and these cars became, almost overnight, a fashionable cult in Britain. With the independant front suspension introduced in 1934 under the name 'Knee-Action', they set a new standard of comfort, and if the steering wheel was a bit woolly, well, that was the chauffeur's worry. In fact the chauffeurs were enthusiastic about them. They performed well and reliably and they were much easier to service than any European car.

If chauffeurs were suggesting a new approach to the whole subject of cars, so the cars were suggesting a new approach to chauffeurs. It was no longer essential that the chauffeur should be a good mechanic. As long as he could drive, looked smart, and was pleasant and polite, that was often considered enough. It was, though, still an advantage if he had some mechanical ability, particularly on country estates where there were various sorts of engine apart from those in cars. Not only things like pumps, but almost anything faintly mechanical, from changing a fuse to hanging a picture, came within the purlieus of a chauffeur's duties. One report details the complicated operation which the chauffeur carried out to floodlight the lawn for dancing (it must have been a very smooth lawn). This was a more or less permanent fixture, erected in May and dismantled in September, but a more extemporary affair took place on another estate one winter.

There had been heavy frosts for some days, and as soon as the ice on the lake was judged to be strong enough the owners hastily got up a dinner party, telling the guests to bring skates.

As soon as they arrived the chauffeurs drove the cars away and parked them in a ring round the lake, so that for the rest of the night the skaters were illuminated by the headlights. It would be interesting to know how many of the cars were able, as dawn came, to start up, and how many had flat batteries.

Chauffeurs were expected to double up as loaders, gillies, caddies, and generally give a helping hand in any sporting activity – even, at one preparatory school, taking part in a chauffeurs' race. Among the qualifications called for in one advertisement was that the applicant for the chauffering job should have a tenor voice to sing in the choir. Cricket featured fairly prominently, and a slow left-hander was more coveted than an expert mechanic who could not bowl.

If a visitor should come without a chauffeur at most country houses his car would be whisked away and washed, and quite often it was filled with petrol as well.

From being a remote specialist, like the piano-tuner or the hair-dresser, who paid regular visits and then departed, the motor expert had developed into the chauffeur, who was an indispensible part of the establishment. He may have lost something of his awe-inspiring mystery, but as the years went by he became more and more integrated with the household and his employers placed increasing dependance upon him.

Strangely enough, it was usually jobs in small households which chauffeurs preferred, partly because of the variety and partly because of the freedom which their authority gave them. Except for the godlike figures of head chauffeurs, the men did not often stay long in positions where they were only one of a large team, unless they were expecting to be promoted when the head chauffeur retired.

There were, however, varying sizes of team, and the smaller ones were considered highly desirable because the tasks of the individual chauffeurs were clearly defined, and confined to duties specifically connected with cars. Delighted to be half of a team of four were the Kenchington brothers, one of whom drove Captain Smith-Bingham and the other his wife. The third chauffeur drove horse-boxes and did the maintenance, while the fourth was in charge of the shooting-brake which was used for short trips such as shopping or taking luggage to the station – except in summer, when it would be taken to a Scottish grouse-moor. The Kenchingtons did not have to concern themselves with anything except the cars, because the staff of thirty-six included an electrician and a carpenter who also did the odd jobs.

Compared with some, a team of four chauffeurs was quite modest. The eleventh Duke of Bedford employed sixteen in the 1920s, and maharajahs had three or four to each car in their fleets. Lady Juliet Duff went to stay with the Duke and Duchess of Portland at Welbeck Abbey in the 1930s and was surprised to be met at the station by a hired car. The driver handed her a note from the Duchess apologizing for sending a hired car but explaining that, 'This afternoon the chauffeurs are playing the Footmen's First Eleven at cricket.'

17

Miss James

In the early days driving a car was considered a male prerogative, though some would amplify the description as a male chauvinist pig prerogative. There were valorous exceptions, like Camille du Gast who entered for the Paris–Madrid race of 1903 and was well up with the leaders when she stopped to give first aid to a team-mate who had crashed. Her contemporaries, however, looked upon her feats as rather like those of Grace Darling – admirable, but not for them.

Motoring, to the elegant, veiled, long-skirted, parasoled Edwardian ladies was a messy enough business when you were a passenger. Personally to conduct the smelly thing was not attractive to them. There was, moreover, a perfectly valid practical reason why they did not take readily to driving, and that was that a great deal of sheer physical strength was required. Imagine swinging a 6-cylinder Napier on a cold morning, or changing the tyre of a 60-horsepower Mercedes one wet night.

Nevertheless, some girls did drive, and around 1910 one big London store had a fleet of vans with a very eye-catching team of female drivers. But it was the First World War which really gave the girls their chance. Those who previously would not have considered earning their livings thought it patriotic to get a job. Those who would have got a job in any case – in factory, shop or, most likely, in domestic service – suddenly found an alternative which might be interesting. With so many chauffeurs away at the war there was plenty of opportunity. There was petrol rationing and many cars were laid up, but still there remained a lot of essential professions, such as doctors, whose whole ability to carry on their work depended on their cars. They were thankful to find somebody – anybody – to drive the things.

It was with a doctor that Fanny Robertson (no relation to Peter) took a job when his chauffeur had been called up. For the four years of the war she battled with the cars, the roads, and the weather in the wilds of Scotland. In wartime conditions the difficulties were formidable. No glossy Daimler or smooth Rolls-Royce to glide about in, but a 1912 Overland (open of course), a curious vehicle called a GWK, and a terrible contraption, Auto Wheel by name, which you bolted to the frame of a push-bike.

Fanny was seventeen years old, but rapidly grew older. In the remote parts of Perthshire the inhabitants had not yet been trained to be ill only at surgery times, and they were likely to call the doctor out at any hour of the twenty-four. Off he would go, with Fanny at the wheel. In the blizzards which sweep over those inhospitable mountains she always took a shovel and a pail full of rags soaked in paraffin. When they came to a snowdrift piling up in the glens she would light a few of the rags and heat the shovel over them to enable it to get through the snow more quickly. If it was foggy she would take a storm lantern, stop the car, and walk a few hundred yards ahead. Then she would put the lantern down, return to the car and drive up to the lantern. For fear of cruising Zeppelins, no headlights were allowed, and she had to make do with smelly oil sidelights.

There were hazards in daylight, too. The GWK had its engine in the middle (you wound it up at the side, like a toy), but its radiator in the conventional place. The pipes from one to the other ran underneath the car, exposed to the mud and all the elements, and on a cold day they froze while she drove along. In fact the whole of the underside of this vehicle was indecently exposed, and all sorts of parts, such as the flywheel, would start slipping in wet weather and have to be dried off with a petrol-soaked rag before Fanny and the doctor could go on.

The petrol itself presented problems. Before daring to put it in the tank she had to filter it most carefully, not only through a fine hair mesh, but through a chamois leather as well. If this was not done the carburettor jets soon became choked. As this was wartime, the petrol, bad as it was, was strictly rationed, and for non-medical errands Fanny had to make use of the Auto Wheel, an ill-balanced and grotesque forerunner of the moped, which was almost unsteerable. It had to be pedalled uphill.

Fanny was a gallant girl, ready for anything, but it was fortunate that less robust ladies were not called upon to be so adventurous. The people most likely to prefer chauffeuses to chauffeurs were usually old ladies living alone, often in seaside places with an equable climate like Bournemouth or Torquay. The driving duties would be minimal, but the chauffeuse would make up a four at bridge and help with the crossword puzzle. This type of job really called more for a companion than a driver, and one divorcee who obtained such a post far preferred gardening to driving. When the old lady died and left her a handsome legacy she sold the car and never drove herself again.

However affluent a society may be, there is always a proportion which falls on hard times, and this makes life particularly difficult for those who have not been trained for any employment. In the nineteenth century there was a ready market for impoverished young ladies to be employed as governesses, and in the twentieth they had the additional option of becoming chauffeuses. Some took kindly to it, others did not. The more introvert ones usually had a wretched time. Servants were wary of them, feeling that the chauffeuse had a foot in both camps, and employers frequently treated them with some ambivalence. They might, for instance, eat with their employers but would not be offered wine unless there were guests present. The children of the household would be instructed to treat the chauffeuse with circumspection. 'We had to refer to her as Miss Muirhead,' writes one correspondent. 'She spoke very little and was rather aloof.'

But the sad ladies suffering silent sorrows were outnumbered by the lively girls who found the whole thing rather a lark. At the beginning of the First World War there was an eighteen-year-old girl who wanted to be a nurse. But she was told that she could not be accepted for training until she was twenty-four, so she decided to fill in the time by becoming a chauffeuse. She found a doctor whose chauffeur was due to be called up two months later, and she spent those two months under his instruction. There were two elderly cars, a Singer and a Rover, and she was taught how to clean the plugs and attend to the greasing.

When the chauffeur departed to the war she took over and, in fact, except for the work carried out by the local garage, she did more to help the doctor than the man had done. He had never expected his chauffeur to show any aptitude as a midwife, but the would-be nurse was a valuable assistant at confinements. She liked the job so much that she remained in it until the doctor died eight years later. She then began her official nursing training, much helped by the experience she had gained while – though not as – a chauffeuse.

Not all apprentice-chauffeuses received a supervised course of instruction. A housemaid at a preparatory school was asked if she would like to become the school chauffeuse, as men were scarce just after the First World War. She was delighted, and an obstacle course was erected on the playing fields so that she could practise manoeuvring with no risk of damaging anything. The chauffeuse at another school was expected to supervise 'prep'.

When the men started to return after demobilization, a chauffeuse was not at all accepted as 'one of the boys', and it was only the most firm-minded ones who continued to compete in what was thought to be very much a man's world. One who did worked for a lady who lived in hotels. Each year she would meet the same chauffeurs at the same hotels and, by 'giving them as good as I got' she maintained her position of independence. In the end they stopped chaffing her and some of them offered to help clean the car, an offer which was courteously but firmly refused.

She noticed that the hotel porters were helpful to the chauffeurs of employers who tipped well, but if they did not the sins of the employers were vented on the chauffeurs. She made sure of getting sufficient help with the heavy cases by arranging with her employer that she should be given the money to distribute the tips.

What the chauffeuse wore depended very much on the employer, and there was not any set pattern of uniform. Some wore skirts, some wore slacks, most wore matching coats and skirts. Some wore ordinary blouses, some shirts with collar and tie. Colour was as varied as it was with men, dark blue, maroon, (or, as one chauffeuse insisted, 'aubergine'), dark green, grey. Hats were either like a chauffeur's – but usually without stiffening round the crown – or 'fore and aft' like an air hostess's. One chauffeuse was allowed to wear her own clothes but made to wear a beret, which she hated; another, who worked for the owner of a dressmaking business, doubled as a model when not actually driving, and usually drove in a light overall and a fur coat.

All these sartorial deviations were swept away with the advent of another war. It was the Second World War which really caused women drivers to come into their own. The very efficient services they performed in the Armed Forces won them respect on all sides. The girls of Britain, from HRH Princess Elizabeth (later HM Queen Elizabeth

II) downwards, flocked to perform the many driving jobs which were needed. Few of them, though, continued as chauffeuses afterwards. An exception was the girl who returned to an office job and then found that she 'soon pined for the freedom which driving gave us'. She applied for, and got, a job with an elderly lady whose Rolls-Royce Phantom III was just being made ready after having been laid up for the duration of the war. The local Rolls-Royce agents put her through a stringent test both of driving and of mechanical knowledge, which she passed quite easily. But what really swung things in her favour was that at the interview she was able to satisfy the employer that she could sew.

One lady who was considered rather on the old side for the Armed Forces took over her husband's taxi service and spent the war and her meagre petrol ration ferrying soldiers from Maresfield camp in Sussex to the delights of nearby towns. Her nocturnal adventures became famous as she careered through the night with blacked-out head-lights, sweeping everything from her path with a stream of invective which brought a blush to the cheek of many a trooper.

A particularly determined girl decided that if she became an ambulance driver she might, at some stage of the Second World War, catch up with her boyfriend who was in the Army. She finally achieved her objective in Brussels a few days after the end of the war. He rounded the whole thing off by proposing to her in the ballroom in which the Duchess of Richmond held her famous ball on the eve of the battle of Waterloo. She accepted, but did not marry him.

It was in the context of the chauffeuse that there arose one of the greatest romances in the twentieth century, indeed in history. It was that between General Dwight D. Eisenhower and Kay Summersby. Kay was a highly intelligent cultured girl who felt that she could best serve her country in time of war by doing something which she was already good at. Accordingly she enrolled as a driver and was soon driving American generals round London. In the bombing and the blackout this was a task which called for all of her skill and courage, qualities which she possessed in abundance.

General Eisenhower was appointed to command the Allied invasion of Europe upon which the outcome of the war, and with it the future of the world, would depend. The planning for this gigantic operation took place in London, and Eisenhower's life became one continuous round of discussions, conferences and decisions, as he weighed up the factors, military, diplomatic and logistic, which would effect the course of this great enterprise. Through it all he had to maintain an unruffled calm, exuding confidence.

Kay was herself of a quality high enough to understand the strains of the responsibility which he bore. She realized the importance of sparing him the addition of little worries and irritations, and she was meticulous in ensuring that the car was always ready for him, exactly where he expected to find it. She studied routes in advance and never made a mistake, estimating with great accuracy the length of time a journey would take.

Gradually General Eisenhower came to understand that he could reply upon her utterly. A less sensitive man might have taken it all for granted, simply thankful that there was one aspect of a busy life which presented no problems. But Eisenhower was not like that. He found time – made time – to get to know his staff. As he came to know Kay better he soon saw that she was a quite outstanding person, and it was not long before they fell in love.

They found a little house on Kingston Hill where they could occasionally snatch a few hours away from the fierce spotlight which beat upon him. Both of them had the power of dissociating themselves from the stupendous concerns which would have overwhelmed a lesser man, so that after even those very few precious hours he was able to return rejuvenated, his confidence and his energy restored.

Even when the war was over, and Eisenhower's need had lessened, the love was as strong and clear as ever. He longed to put the relationship on a permanent footing, but it was not to be. General Marshall, the United States Chief of Staff, wrote him a letter in the sternest possible terms, and Eisenhower made the agonizing decision to give Kay up. It was a rare occasion, one on which honour and duty did not march in step.

But although the glamour of Kay Summersby's romance singles her out, she was by no means alone. Hundreds of girls drove staff cars and ambulances, and today most of the official Government drivers are women.

In sharp contrast to Kay was the girl who drove an admiral. She was much in awe of this remote majestic figure, terrified of being the recipient of one of his shattering broadsides. She was thankful that he always sat in the back of the limousine, isolated by the glass partition.

One day she was ordered to drive him from Portsmouth to London. She looked up the route, which included the old coaching road along the Hog's Back. It was an easy way, but she memorized it carefully, because in the war all signposts had been removed at the first threat of invasion. All went well, and she was making good time on the straight deserted road when there was a tap on the partition and the admiral told her to stop. She pulled in and he alighted, wandering off into a clump of trees some distance behind the car, evidently bent on attending to a call of nature. She sat waiting for a few minutes until it occurred to her that she too might be prudent to do something similar. It was still quite a long way to London, and she had better take the opportunity while she had it.

Accordingly, she slipped out of the driving seat and looked round for a bush. The nearest was a hundred yards or so in front of the car, and she made for it. Conscious that the admiral had started several minutes before she had, and anxious not to keep him waiting, she did what she wanted as quickly as possible and scuttled back to the car. She slipped into the driving seat, started up, and drove off, relieved that there had been no delay to occasion a bellow of wrath from behind the glass.

There was little traffic, and after a smooth, fast journey she drew up at the Admiralty well ahead of schedule. She jumped down and opened the door of the rear compartment. But instead of the ample figure of the admiral heaving himself off the seat, the passenger compartment was empty. She stared in disbelief. The admiral, she asked herself, where was he? The answer was painfully clear. Still on the Hog's Back, where she had left him.

18

Friend James

It would be agreeable if one could draw sociological conclusions from the relationships between employers and their chauffeurs. But it is not possible, beyond observing that nice people behaved nicely and nasty people behaved nastily. There are cases where employers treated chauffeurs with inconsiderateness amounting almost to cruelty; there are cases of chauffeurs who took their employers for a ride figuratively as well as literally. There are employers who complain that they never had an honest chauffeur; there are chauffeurs who never had a satisfactory employer.

There is, however, overwhelming evidence to show that when there came together a chauffeur and an employer who suited one another the relationship became very satisfactory indeed. The case of David Knowles, who remained chauffeur to the same family for fifty years from the age of eighteen, is by no means unique. Chauffeurs who were fortunate enough to start with a good job, and wise enough to stay with it, had happy lives. It was those who went from job to job, never settling into any one, who found chauffeuring a frustrating career.

Many of the chauffeurs who found a secure job for live integrated themselves with the lives of the family for whom they worked. Their employment became a way of life to them. The payment of 'overtime' was unheard of until a few years ago, and chauffeurs were perfectly happy to be almost permanently on call. The majority of employers granted a day and a half, a day, or at least half a day off per week, in which Sundays were almost always included, and two weeks' holiday a year. However, the chauffeur's working day was much easier than this would suggest, particularly in the country. Few chauffeurs were required to drive for more than a few hours each day, there was plenty of time to do the necessary cleaning and maintenance, and the various odd jobs seldom took very long.

This is not to say that a chauffeur usually had time hanging on his hands. The very nature of chauffeuring attracted enterprising men who were not content to sit about doing nothing. Most chauffeurs were skilled at making things, and there are countless stories of ingenious toys being made for children of employers, and there was one chauffeur to a surgeon who fashioned from wood such a perfect skeleton of a leg that it was used for demonstrations in the teaching hospital.

So many chauffeurs served succeeding generations of the same family that they had to be infinitely adaptable. They might oil the wheels of a perambulator and still be only halfway through their working life when they were servicing the one-time occupant's new MG. Even more of a contrast was when the chauffeur accustomed to conducting a creaking and ancient Daimler limousine, emitting a stately cloud of blue smoke from its slapping sleeve valves, found himself having to drive a Frazer-Nash open sports car home at three o'clock in the morning because the young owner ('For God's sake don't tell the parents') was too drunk to be trusted.

The chauffeurs who had established their positions in the household frequently acted as intermediaries between parents and offspring, sometimes siding with one, sometimes with the other. The good ones were adept at exercising an authority which they did not possess but which they did not hesitate to use. A lady well into middle age still remembers the bitter humiliation she experienced at the hands, or rather the tongue, of her parents' chauffeur. Alighting from the car outside the Savoy, she made some cheeky reply to a request of her mother. The mother was mortified by this public impertinence and, without another word, hastened into the hotel. The daughter was on the point of following her when the chauffeur stepped in front of her and told her exactly what he thought of her behaviour. As the little girl became pinker and pinker the doormen and other chauffeurs gathered round to hear this majestic stream of reproof which the chauffeur timed to halt as the first tear sprang to the little girl's eye. It was a lesson which she never forgot, and thirty years later was able to write with deep emotion of the effect which the example of this wise and decent man had had on her life.

The chauffeur often played a big part in the life of his employer's children. Quite apart from the fascination of the mysterious things the chauffeur could do with machinery, he was somebody a little removed from the house and the people in it, and yet not so far distant that he could not fully comprehend the implications of the storms in the teacups. 'I fled to him when my grandmother became too much for me,' is the memory of how a chauffeur alleviated the loneliness of one little girl. Another child, an orphan, was brought up by a spinster who had a chauffeur called Barwick. He used to fetch her from school and do most of the maths homework for her on the way. When she grew up and got married and had a daughter of her own, she discovered that the child was surprised to find that a little friend had a something called a 'grandpa' to go with her granny. She had previously thought that everybody, like herself, had a Granny and a Barwick.

Little boys, no less than little girls, often regarded the family chauffeur as a cross between a father confessor and an umpire. This attitude was by no means confined to English children. In Westchester County, New York, Henry the chauffeur watched over the son of the house in a paternal way and finally taught him to drive. One of the precepts he made a great point of was never to drink and drive, and it was one which he never broke himself. His pupil, however, was not quite quick enough to learn.

'I recall one evening I took a girl I was interested in to a dance,' he said years later. 'I don't know how it happened, but I had a bit too much to drink. She complained. I argued and she went home with another guy. I was sore and had to drive home alone. On the way back I didn't feel too well, and pulled off the road to take a nap. How Henry found me I never discovered. But the next morning he asked me to come to him.

'He looked me in the eye, not unkindly but, I felt, with the clout of the Recording Angel. "You made an idiot of yourself out there last night," he said, "and if you don't know it I'm telling you now. I'm trying to patch up with this girl and maybe I can. I want your co-operation, and you are *not to drive for one month* – not anything, any time, anywhere, for any reason. If you do and I learn of it you will be a very sorry young man. But if you do as I say, in one month I'll forget everything that happened last night because you'll have learned your lesson."

'Henry watched me like a hawk and he kept his word. One month later I really believe he forgot what had happened. I don't know what he ever said to the young lady, but it was effective. I was forgiven and eventually we were married.'

An escapade which did not have such a romantic ending took place in England. Again, it was a case in which the chauffeur taught the son of the house to drive and was pleased with his pupil's progress. The pupil's father, on the other hand, did not share his chauffeur's enthusiasm, and issued strict instructions that on no account was his offspring to be allowed to drive the family limousine, which he regarded as his personal property, not to be used by anybody else except, by an act of condescension, his wife.

In due course the son confided to the chauffeur that he was going to take a girl to a dance – a very special girl to a very special dance. What a pity, he said, that he would have to go in the old two-seater with the flapping hood and the broken sidescreens. If only his father had not vetoed the use of the limousine! It was not, he meant to say, as if he was a wild driver, and he promised not to drink. Still, it was no good wishing. His father had forbidden him to drive the limousine, and that was that. Except, he added thoughtfully, his father would never know. Well, he wouldn't, would he? He would be away on a business trip.

The chauffeur was a kind-hearted man, and he was as little able to resist the steady pressure as is a stone to resist the incessant drip of water. The young man behaved impeccably. He had no drink all evening, he delivered the girl safely back to her parents, he coasted down the drive so as not to awaken the household, he put the car away and went to bed.

When the chauffeur went to clean the car next morning he was relieved, though not surprised, to find no scratches, no dents, no exterior damage. It was when he opened the rear door that his eyes and nose told him that one of the less restrained dancers had used the limousine as a 'vomitorium'. The smell was finally vanquished by liberal sprayings with lavender water, but the dark stain on the dove-grey cloth of the back seat resisted all attempts to remove it. When he set off to meet his employer at the station the chauffeur was not feeling too good himself.

The employer bustled out of the station in excellent spirits. He had had a successful trip and he was glad to be home. As he got into the car he noticed that the seat was covered with a neatly folded rug, something which had never happened before. When he enquired the reason the chauffeur explained that during the long train journey it was quite likely that his employer's coat might have picked up a smut and he was taking no chances of marking the car's upholstery. The employer was amused, but pleased to have yet more evidence of the concern his chauffeur felt for the well-being of his charge.

It was a brilliant short-term solution, but the stain did not dry out. The son and the chauffeur were gloomily aware that the day of reckoning must come. It was not long before their nerve cracked and they decided that there was nothing for it but to own up and accept the punishment. Disaster was unavoidable.

And then the son had an idea. It might soften the blow a little if the confession came not direct from himself and the chauffeur but from his own mother. The chauffeur agreed, and together they approached the employer's wife. This intelligent woman immediately grasped the gravity of the situation. But, to their astonishment, she produced a solution. She would take her husband abroad for a short holiday and while they were away the car could go to the coachbuilder's and have the seat re-upholstered.

The deception worked perfectly but, like many otherwise perfect crimes, it failed when one of the conspirators talked. Much to their surprise however, the employer took it fairly mildly, adopting a resigned attitude and feeling that he and his chauffeur had both been victims of exploitation.

Many chauffeurs enjoyed teaching their employers' children to drive, taking a proprietorial interest in their progress, but Peter Robertson was not one of them. After his original employer's death, he remained in the service of the son, a man a few years younger than himself. By the time the next generation was old enough to have a licence Peter would be near retiring age but, it was thought, he would like to stay on for another year to give the instruction. But it was not to be. The two boys had been given bicycles for Christmas some years earlier, and had gone to bed leaving the new cycles lying in the drive. Peter was so shocked at this maltreatment of machinery that he announced that 'when the first of those wee bairns is old enough to drive a car I'll be awa' tae Blairgowrie.' And when the boy reached seventeen awa' tae Blairgowrie Peter went.

Another plan for tuition by a chauffeur was prudently withdrawn. A young couple engaged as chauffeur and cook a couple of servants the same age as themselves. The employer's wife greatly appreciated the driving lessons given her by the handsome young chauffeur but what she really wanted was to be taught to ride his motor cycle. But she came to the conclusion that the only way to learn would be to sit on the pillion with her arms round his waist and, she said sorrowfully, 'I didn't think my husband would like that. And I didn't think my cook would like it, either.'

These were, however, exceptions. By far the most usual thing was for the chauffeur to teach the children of the house to drive. Apart from his specialized knowledge, he had probably known them since nursery days and they had come to respect him and do what he told them. And the rapport between the chauffeur and the employer's children was often echoed by the relationship between the chauffeur's children and the employer and his wife. In some cases the wife even acted as baby-sitter when the chauffeur and his wife were out on his day off.

On one Gloucestershire estate the chauffeur's son shared driving instruction with the son of the house. This was in the early 1920s, when radio (known as 'wireless' then) was in its infancy. The chauffeur made a crystal set, and after dinner the young people from 'the House' would crowd into the small sitting room of the chauffeur's flat to listen to its squawks.

Living on an estate as this, the chauffeur's family enjoyed many benefits. The chauffeur's daughter remembers a happy childhood. 'There were fresh vegetables twice a week, and a bunch of flowers most weeks of the year. In the summer we would be allowed to pick surplus fruit for preserving. We also had plenty of milk every day from the dairy. There was a large coalshed which I never saw empty, and we could fetch logs when we needed them. As the garages were centrally heated, our flat above had radiators in the hall and bedrooms. All interior decorating was done for us. We did not have a garden of our own but we were allowed to go round the grounds and woods. Mother was told by the employer that the garden was there for her enjoyment as much as for his.

'For some years the employer's wife was President of the Women's Institute and my mother a committee member. It was almost accepted that Father was a member, as he took them to meetings, met visiting speakers, ran the projector for film shows, and helped in many ways.'

The chauffeur was at his employer's bedside when he died, and although he was himself due to enter hospital for major surgery that same week he insisted on postponing it for a couple of days so that he could be a bearer at his employer's funeral.

A happier occasion was when a 78-year-old chauffeur emerged from retirement in order to drive to his christening a member of the fifth generation of the family which he had served so faithfully and so long.

Tears of deep emotion were running down the old man's cheeks and the car pursued an erratic course but, nevertheless, the short journey was successfully accomplished, a touching demonstration of loyalty and friendship on both sides.

Good employers always showed consideration for their chauffeurs, and the consideration was extended to the families, with medical treatment and education provided in times of need. As one employer told his chauffeur, 'In times of prosperity you look after us. In times of adversity we look after you.'

But it was not always the chauffeur who suffered the times of adversity. Of one employer the chauffeur wrote, 'I met my boss several months later and the poor chap never had the cash to treat me to a cup of tea.'

Another couple who found themselves in reduced – though not desperate – circumstances in the Depression of the early 1930s had as cook and chauffeur a brother and sister. One evening the cook came to them and announced that she and her brother had been discussing the position and had come to the conclusion that the family could no longer afford to employ them both. Her brother could easily find another job but that would leave the elderly employers without anyone to drive them. She therefore proposed that her brother should stay on long enough to teach her to drive so that when he went she could take on his duties as well as her own.

That chauffeur found that his job came to an end in an orderly manner, but a rather more abrupt finale was when a chauffeur stood and watched his bankrupt employer's Rolls-Royce being towed away by the broker's men.

Sometimes it was triumph not disaster which brought a chauffeur's employment to an end – when the employer was promoted to some official position in which a car and chauffeur were supplied. One such appointment was that of Henry Montgomery-Campbell, Bishop of Guildford, to be Bishop of London. He found a new job for his own chauffeur, William Betts, and made sure that seats were reserved for him and his wife at the enthronement. At the close of the solemn service the procession was returning to the vestry when the Bishop caught his ex-chauffeur's eye and gave him a broad wink.

He had long before worked out a code with William Betts. If after spending the evening at some vicarage in the Guildford diocese he found it difficult to get away from a talkative parson, he would slowly

Not all chauffeur-driven cars were sedate limousines. Kenneth Kenchington with a 4½-litre Bentley.

When open, a landaulette could give a passenger sunstroke and a stiff neck simultaneously.

Real chauffeurs were seldom as handsome as film stars. *Merrily We Live* (1938), in which Brian Aherne played a writer who is mistaken for a tramp and engaged as a chauffeur. (Kobal Collection)

Eric von Stroheim played chauffeur to Gloria Swanson in the eerie *Sunset Boulevard* (1950). William Holden is her passenger. (Kobal Collection)

John Williams and Audrey Hepburn in *Sabrina Fair*. Actors did not take their coats off as often as did real chauffeurs. (Kobal Collection)

Robert Shaw and Sarah Miles in the 1973 film *The Hireling*. (Kobal Collection)

Male Hollywood stars thought it more glamorous to drive their own cars. Actresses had no such inhibitions about employing chauffeurs. This is Jean Harlow's beside her V-12 cylinder Cadillac.

Owners might consider foreign cars, such as this Isotta Fraschini, to be rather dashing, but chauffeurs considered a Daimler or a Rolls-Royce to be more dignified.

ABOVE LEFT: A chauffeur's lot may have been a happy one but it entailed a great deal of waiting, waiting, waiting. Ascot, 1932.

ABOVE RIGHT: Pride of place. (Thurston Hopkins)

BELOW LEFT: Severe petrol rationing meant that chauffeurs had to make do with humbler transport than the customary Rolls-Royce. Maurice Harbord, chauffeur to the Burnaby-Atkins family of Tolethorpe Hall, Lincolnshire, with a 1940 Hillman Minx. One headlight is blacked out, the other disconnected. (J. M. Harbord)

BELOW RIGHT: The two Praters, father and son, photographed at Neville Chamberlain's memorial service in front of the Duke of Gloucester's Rolls-Royce Phantom III, which was at that time chauffeured by Prater Jr, while his father was chauffeuring Anthony Eden.

ABOVE LEFT: Michael McAdam, by courtesy of whom this photograph is reproduced, was one of the last chauffeurs to wear traditional tunic and breeches in the late 1960s.

ABOVE RIGHT: Lavinia Legard, a hire chauffeuse with her own Rolls-Royce. Reproduced by courtesy of Lavinia Legard.

BELOW: Elegance in white. Rolls-Royce, chauffeur and Marlene Dietrich all match in *Paris When It Sizzles*. (Kobal Collection)

Still proudly serving the Duke of Gloucester. William Prater drives Prince Henry's son after his wedding.

Even when it has been only from Buckingham Palace to Clarence House, Her Majesty's car is cleaned every time it has been out.

Barbara Cartland and her chauffeur, photographed by Patrick Lichfield.

New Yorker cartoon by Charles Addams.

"Now that we've given up the car, I wonder if we still need Orkins."

move his hand to and fro. This was the signal for Betts to draw smoothly away, gradually gathering speed. Another custom agreed between them was that after a visit to a vicarage where the host was too shy to offer the use of the lavatory Betts would stop at the first field containing a haystack.

The whole question of urination caused a tremendous amount of fuss, and few chauffeur-employer combinations seem to have solved it as sensibly as the Bishop and Betts. Some employers simply would not allow their chauffeurs to stop, and this meant highly unpleasant manoeuvres involving jars and bottles. In the United States there was a device delicately known as 'the chauffeur's leg', which consisted of a pipe which could be clipped to the seat when not in use and which led to a tin box on the floor. Among the more idiotic euphemisms was the one used by the parents of a little girl who told her, whenever the chauffeur stopped and disappeared into a field, that he had gone to look for a robin's nest. This simply confirmed, in a reasonable child's mind, that the chauffeur was mad to interrupt the journey in order to pursue his ornithological hobby, and that her parents were mad to permit it. When, years later, she discovered the truth she saw no reason to alter her opinion that her parents were mad, and to the opinion that the chauffeur was mad she added the opinion that he had a weak bladder.

Although there are many examples of employers who appeared to think that chauffeurs could withhold their urine at will, there were others who expected them to produce it on demand. In the early days when headlights used carbide gas, water was needed to create it, and when the supply dried up during a nocturnal journey the chauffeur was expected to replenish it from his own resources.

Another matter for which there was no definite custom was what the employers should call their chauffeurs, although there was a set form for what the chauffeurs should call them. When speaking to the employer, the chauffeur would refer to the latter's wife as 'Her Grace', 'Her Ladyship', or, if she had no title, 'Madam'. To the wife he would refer to her husband as 'His Grace', 'His Lordship', 'Sir George', or, if untitled, 'The Master'. It is a curious thing that female servants more usually referred to the employer's wife as 'The Mistress', while male servants used 'Madam'. Among themselves the servants referred to their employers as 'The Family' or 'The People'. Even unpopular employers were seldom given really uncomplimentary nicknames. A young chauffeur who entered the service of a ghastly old millionairess in London's Egerton Gardens was surprised to find that in a basement seething with discontent she was rarely called anything worse than "Er Upstairs'.

Employers, however, did not have any fixed rule about addressing their chauffeurs. Some used the man's surname, some the Christian name. In the days when footmen had been plentiful, some large households had the habit of always calling the first footman by the same name, regardless of how many holders of that office there had been since. If the first one was called John all his successors would be called John, and in some houses the changing population of house-maids was always known as Jane and Mary. Chauffeurs, however, seem to have escaped this strange form of identification, and been permitted to retain their own names. But there was no rhyme or reason about it. Peter Robertson, for instance, was invariably called Peter, whereas the 'country' chauffeur to the same family was always addressed by his surname.

Some employers found it embarrassing to call new servants by their Christian names, particularly in days when forms of address were in general highly stylized. It was a relief when the servant turned out to have a name which could be either, like Stuart, Leslie, or James. Another version of the story quoted on the title page – and probably equally apochryphal – is that of a Duchess whose chauffeur was on holiday and who had a temporary replacement supplied by an agency.

'And what is your name?' she enquired when he collected her at Claridges.

'James, Your Grace.'

'Christian name or surname?'

'Christian name, Your Grace.'

'Oh. Well I would prefer to use your surname. What is it?'

'Darling.'

'Drive on, James.'

19

Really James?

It is a regrettable fact that chauffeurs have not been well served by songwriters. Other servants have inspired the Muse, but not chauffeurs. There does not seem to be any reason for this neglect, for surely a chauffeur keeping a rare store of oil and tyres is as worthy of acclaim as Old Simon the Cellarer with his rare store of Malmsey and Malvoisie. John Thomas, too, was a butler not a chauffeur.

> He was the pride of the servant's hall,
> In his red plush breeches
> In his red plush breeches
> That kept John Thomas warm.

In fact, the red plush breeches suggest a footman, not a butler, but whatever he was he was not a chauffeur. Though how easy it would have been to make him one by exchanging the red plush for blue whipcord breeches.

One cannot, of course, blame Shakespeare for neglecting chauffeurs because they did not exist in his time. This is really a tragedy, because otherwise we might have had Romeo's chauffeur sharing the stage with Juliet's Nurse. But there is less excuse for those poets who actually employed chauffeurs. Rudyard Kipling, for instance, observed that 'half a proper gardener's work is done upon his knees', and he might just as well have taken note of the chauffeur crawling under the car.

It was left to George Bernard Shaw to create a fully-rounded character in the form of a chauffeur. He was early in on the act, indeed so early that the word 'chauffeur' was not yet in common parlance, and

Shaw qualifies it as 'chauffeur or automobilist or motorer or whatever England may presently decide to call him'. However uncertain the nomenclature may have been, there is the usual Shavian sharpness about the delineation of the portrait. His employer sums up the chauffeur's attitude succintly. 'He positively likes the car to break down because it brings out my gentlemanly helplessness and his workmanlike skill and resource.'

The employer's friend backs him up with the comment, 'I believe most intensely in the dignity of labour,' to which the chauffeur makes the crushing reply, 'That's because you never done any.'

This character, Henry Straker, appears in *Man and Superman*, set in 1901–1903, and is described as a 'momentous social phenomenon'. Shaw has immortalized the type of young man who was attracted to motoring in its beginnings. Straker, we are told, was trained at a Polytechnic and is symptomatic of the rising class of intelligent, unmoneyed youth with a scientific bent. 'Here have we literary and cultured persons been for years setting up a cry of the "New Woman" whenever some unusually old-fashioned female came along, and never noticing the advent ot the "New Man",' remarks one of the other characters in the play. 'Straker's the New Man.'

Unfortunately Shaw never returned to the theme of the chauffeur, and we have to be content with his *pointilliste* description of a very early one. It is a pity that he never drew a portrait of his own chauffeur, Fred Day, who was with him for thirty-one years and who regarded him with affectionate and tolerant amusement. 'Mr and Mrs Shaw were both unorthodox people,' he comments in discreet understatement.

Possibly Shaw felt that there was danger in portraying Day. Engaging though his mischievous wit was when spoken, if committed to paper it might have corroded an easy relationship.

One novelist who endured anything but an easy relationship with his chauffeur got his own back by creating a chauffeur so evil that it defeated its own object. The character was so awful that it cannot have occurred to anybody that a real chauffeur could be remotely like that. But no doubt it relieved some of the resentment the author felt towards his employee, whose wife was the cook. The author was a timid man and could not face the appalling row that would have taken place if he had sacked them, nor the subsequent inconvenience of a servantless widower household. 'Make yourself ten feet tall,' the employer of a large staff told him, speaking from the depths of her own experience.

A fictional chauffeur who bears little resemblance to reality is the one after whom L. P. Hartley's novel *The Hireling* is entitled. Like Lady Chatterley's Lover, his form of employment is used mainly as an indication of his social status; there is little description of a life typical of one who followed that particular trade.

Somerset Maugham could have given us a marvellous picture of a chauffeur if he had wished. With his genius for basing fictional characters on real people, we might have had a lifelike picture of his French chauffeur, Jean, a merry man who served for many years at the Villa Mauresque. Incidentally, the social life on Cap Ferrat seems to have been just as hectic for the servants as for the rich and famous, with caretakers throwing lavish parties in the absence of their employers.

But perhaps the greatest regret of all is that P. G. Wodehouse did not turn his attention to chauffeurs. It is true that there is a rather wooden character called Voules operating in this capacity at Blandings Castle, but his existence can only be due to the fact that nobody could imagine Lord Emsworth or Lady Constance driving a car. Voules never begins to approach the studied character drawing which was lavished on Beach, the butler who was that 'stately procession of one'. The Bertie Wooster stories do not call for chauffeurs, and the nearest they get to it is when Bertie is giving the wheel of the old two-seater a thoughtful twirl and Jeeves is sitting impassively beside him. But it is made quite clear that Jeeves is there in his capacity of gentleman's gentleman rather than chauffeur, and to point the distinction he wears a bowler hat.

One author who does, fortunately, give us a lot about chauffeurs is Dornford Yates. He was exceptionally well qualified to do so because it was he who ghosted Stamper's book about his employment with King Edward VII. The splendid fictional characters Bell and Rowley who served Jonah Mansel and Richard Chandos so faithfully were excellent drivers, skilled mechanics and utterly reliable servants, loyal to the core. Stamper himself, that most devoted of men, would have approved of them wholeheartedly. When beset by villains on every side they would take time off to 'berth the Rolls' behind the double doors of some secluded barn and remove from it all traces of the Transylvanian dust which had accumulated as it dashed to and fro on its errands of mercy. This was conduct well in accordance with the chauffeur tradition, though whether they did not perhaps exceed the call of duty when, at the instigation of their employers, they assisted in the wholesale wiping out of the opposition, is arguable.

The other Dornford Yates chauffeur, Fitch, never went to those lengths. Whenever he makes an appearance, as he does throughout the 'Berry' books, he is a model of what a chauffeur should be. Apart from his impeccable behaviour, he was always game for anything, such as driving from the West End of London to the Albert Hall in a pea-soup fog with Bob Pleydell walking in front and burning his hand on the oil side-lamp which he carried. This incident is so like a true one related in Stamper's book that it is easy to see how Dornford Yates may have got the idea.

An even more remarkable blending of fact and fiction between a real chauffeur and an imaginary one took place around 1907 in Bradford. A likely lad called David Knowles worked in a garage in the city, and was chosen to drive a van round the stage of the local theatre during the performance of Cinderella. Quite what part the van played in the pantomime is not clear – possibly the coach after it turned into a pumpkin – nor is it clear if the van was eponymous with the leading lady, Florrie Ford. But what is quite clear is that David Knowles was not sufficiently stage struck to be deflected from his chosen career. As soon as he reached eighteen he obtained a job as chauffeur to a doctor, and remained in the employment of the same family until he retired half a century later.

20

Sh!

One of the most highly prized attributes in a chauffeur was discretion. It was inevitable that chauffeurs should hear secrets, and it was a relief to employers to know that they did not have to be too careful about what they said in front of a man who would keep to himself whatever he heard. Though probably few employers achieved quite the supreme disregard of the extrovert Duke who was quarrelling with his mistress in the back of a hired car. To emphasize his point he raised his voice to a near bellow.

'Sh,' said the mistress, jerking her head in the direction of the chauffeur, who was avidly watching in the mirror. 'He'll hear you.' The Duke snorted with impatience. 'Oh for God's sake don't be so bloody middle-class!' he said.

Other passengers, less inhibited, used strategems such as whispers or speaking in French (a chauffeur who had spent four years in Paris found this amusing), but these little devices simply served to draw attention. Employers who took their chauffeurs into their confidence saved themselves a lot of trouble and often found themselves rewarded by loyalty. Sometimes the loyalty verged on the conspiratorial, as in the case of the man who pulled out his wallet as he left the car at his office.

'Go to that flower shop in Victoria Street and spend this.' He handed the chauffeur a note. 'Take them to Mrs ———. You know the address. This is for you,' he added, taking another note from his wallet.

The chauffeur went and bought the flowers, but as he was leaving the shop carrying the large bunch he almost bumped into his employer's wife.

'Good morning, my lady,' he said. 'What a pity you've seen me. His lordship wanted these to be a surprise for you.'

Chauffeurs were usually given a 'float' for expenses, and were often asked to produce money for their employers, as when a man on his way to a funeral made a detour to buy a top hat. After choosing it he found that he had not enough money on him so, accompanied by the assistant, he came out to the car to ask the chauffeur for money. While counting out the correct amount he chucked the new hat on to the back seat. Then he went back into the shop to collect his old hat. When he came out again he was rather fussed, being afraid he would be late for the funeral. He jumped into the car and flung himself down on the seat – and on to the intervening hat. The chauffeur, to his immense credit, preserved an impassive expression.

It was comforting to employers to know that in times of crisis the loyal chauffeur could be relied upon to rally round, often displaying hitherto unsuspected skills, like knowing how to take a wasps' nest, or being good at climbing on to the roof when a chimney caught fire. One employer had the reassuring knowledge that his chauffeur had come to him with a reference from his previous employer saying that he was 'good in ambushes'.

This particular recommendation, which had been earned during the 'Troubles' in Ireland, was never put to the test, but another chauffeur was able to demonstrate how deeply he held the 'Family's' interest at heart. It was just after the end of the Second World War. The chauffeur had been too old to serve in the Armed Forces and had doubled up as butler. To help him a young lad had been engaged while awaiting his call-up. Petrol rationing was very strict and there was little driving to be done, but the chauffeur had his hands full with running a large house.

The employers decided to celebrate the end of the war by giving a party. They had treasured the last of their champagne for this great day, and they made elaborate arrangements for their guests to give each other lifts and so to eke out the meagre amount of petrol available.

Returning a large house to peace-time occupation was a mammoth task, and they were all kept busy – in fact too busy to notice that the teenage daughter was having a torrid love affair with the boy footman. When it did come to light, two days before the party, he was immediately sent packing, some of the precious petrol being used to transport him to his home forty miles away. The daughter, whose name was Alice, was put on to unpacking and washing the champagne glasses, the silver, the china, in the hope of taking her mind off the shattered romance. A few hours before the party was due to begin her mother called her to discuss some small detail, but Alice did not reply. A search disclosed that she was not in the house, and the chauffeur came, white-faced, from the garage, to announce that the Ford Eight was missing.

They held a hasty council of war. It was clear that Alice had fled to her demon lover. In this grave situation there was one ray of hope, which was that she might not get there, for the Ford had not enough petrol to complete the journey. There was, therefore, a slim chance that instant pursuit might be successful. Neither the father nor mother could drive, but they had complete trust in their chauffeur.

'Is there enough petrol in the Rolls?' the mother asked anxiously.

'Just, my lady.' What the chauffeur did not disclose was that although there was enough petrol to get to the ex-footman's home, there certainly was not enough to get back. It was a mission from which there could be no hope of return. Undaunted, he set out.

The hours dragged slowly by, and the first guests began to arrive. For such a joyous occasion they found their hosts curiously distrait, and enquiries for Alice were met with evasive answers. The champagne, too, was not all it might be. It had been kept too long and was slightly flat. But never mind, everyone said; the war was over, and that was all that mattered. They plunged into merry conversation.

If the weather had any sense of occasion it would have been pelting with rain, but instead of a sombre background this human drama was played out in brilliant sunshine beneath a sky of flawless blue. More guests arrived, and the whole party moved out on to the terrace. There was clinking of glasses, and laughter.

Then suddenly the hubbub died, and a great silence fell as all the heads turned towards the drive. Up it trudged the weary figure of the chauffeur with, slung like a sack of potatoes over his shoulder, the inert form of Alice.

Loyalty was, of course, a two-way affair, and if a chauffeur felt that his service was not appreciated he moved on to another job. This occurred with a man who took an enormous pride in keeping his cars impeccably. He was employed by a company to drive the Mercedes which was exclusively used by the chairman. One Monday morning the chairman brought the car back, after driving it himself over the week-end, and the chauffeur was horrified to see an ugly scratch all down one side. He suggested taking it immediately to the coachbuilder for a re-spray.

'Oh no,' said the chairman. 'That would cost the earth. In six weeks' time the shareholders will be buying me a new car, so we'll put up with it until then.'

The chairman might have been prepared to put up with it, the chauffeur said, but he himself would feel ashamed to be seen in a car in that condition. The chairman, therefore, must kindly accept a week's notice.

The chairman's wife, as soon as she heard of it, offered to double the chauffeur's wages if he would stay. He thanked her politely, but declined. He was sorry to leave, he said, and she had always treated him well. But, really, he could not bring himself to remain any longer in the service of a man as mean as her husband. Good afternoon.

It is always admirable, though seldom beneficial, to make a stand on a matter of principle. But to reach the heights of magnificence a gesture must include, beside the elements of self-destruction, a good measure of sheer malignant irresponsibility, a contemptuous abrogation of bounden duty. Such an act was performed by a young chauffeur employed by a querulous and extremely fat old woman. One wet afternoon she was returning home accompanied by a friend of equally generous proportions, when the chauffeur felt the ominous lurch which indicated an expiring tyre, so he brought the car to a halt. A bombardment of questions from the back seat demanded to know what was the matter. The chauffeur patiently explained that one of the rear tyres had been punctured.

To the accompaniment of a steady stream of abuse he took the jack from the boot and set it under the rear spring. It was not a very good jack and it required all his strength to raise the car a few inches. The rain was trickling down the back of his neck, and he felt that he had a cold coming on. He straightened up and approached the side window. Would the ladies, he asked, be good enough to dismount? It would make lifting the car easier and would obviate any danger of the car falling off the jack. He was met with indignant refusal and renewed abuse.

At that moment headlights appeared over the brow of the hill. 'Stop that car,' commanded the employer, 'and tell them to take me home.'

The chauffeur stepped out into the road and held up his hand. The oncoming vehicle slowed down, and he saw that it was not a car but a bus. He hopped on it and was borne away.

A similar humiliation was suffered by a Foreign Secretary, famed for his short temper and long drinks. His chauffeur simply walked away from a broken-down car one day, and went on walking until the Foreign Secretary's roars of rage died away in the distance.

That was undoubtedly game, set, and match to the chauffeur, even though it involved the ultimate sanction of dismissal, but the effect of the gesture would diminish as the sense of outrage faded. For the most hauntingly permanent wound the laurels must go not to a chauffeur, but to the wife of one. Moreover she and her husband had already given notice from the jobs which they had held – he as chauffeur, she as cook, for fourteen years – so she had nothing to lose. It was at the end of the acrimonious farewells that she administered to her erstwhile employer the *coup de grace*.

'And another thing,' she said. 'Since I've been in this house there's never been a plate washed. The dogs have licked them all.'

21

' 'Tis a Mad World, My Masters'

John Taylor

The Great English Eccentric is now an endangered species, its habitat eroded by inflation. For what the English Eccentric needs, if it is to flourish, is an environment of leisure and money. Fortunately, in the Golden Age of Motoring, there was no shortage of either.

As a race, the English have always been rather proud of their eccentrics, endlessly relating stories of their dottiness. Part of the fascination of the eccentric is his utter and complete disregard for what anybody thinks of him. He is genuinely and completely uninterested in public opinion. The other part of the fascination is that there is a sort of indisputable logic underlying all his actions, bizarre as they may seem.

But the eccentric is best enjoyed at one remove. Eccentrics are like tigers: fascinating to observe, but wise men do not get too close to them. Chauffeurs, however, had no option if their employer was an eccentric. They simply had to go along with the fantasy, enduring looking ridiculous as best they could. The heart bleeds for the chauffeur of the employer who complained that the seat of his car was not as comfortable as his favourite armchair, and that the thick pillars obscured his view of the countryside. These were perfectly sensible complaints, and the chauffeur had no difficulty in agreeing that they were valid.

It was only when the employer decided that he must do something about it that the trouble began. For the solution he arrived at bore all the hallmarks of genuine eccentricity. The vehicle he selected fulfilled both the conditions he stipulated. His favourite armchair could be loaded aboard and bolted to the floor. That was one problem solved. The answer to the other was that, sitting high up, he had a perfectly splendid view of the surrounding countryside, quite unimpeded by intrusive pillars. The vehicle was a hearse.

It would be interesting to know whether it was as a result of the acquisition of the hearse that the chauffeur earned, in the employer's awe-stricken family, the sobriquet of 'Drunken George'.

The eleventh Duke of Bedford is often cited as a true eccentric because of his habit of changing cars, in the way that his ancestors had changed horses, half-way between Woburn and London. But, at best he can only be regarded as a borderline case, at least on the evidence of the changing of the cars. The object was not to spare tired cars, but because the Woburn-based chauffeurs did not have the encyclopaedic knowledge of London possessed by those who never travelled farther north than Hendon. If you happen to have twelve or fourteen chauffeurs in your employ, as did this Duke, you can hardly be considered eccentric if you allot them the tasks for which they are best fitted.

If not a true eccentric, he was at least a very fussy man. Whenever he planned to go anywhere by road he would despatch a chauffeur to reconnoitre the way the day before, and only after this dry run would the Duke consent to venture into the unknown. If not proof of eccentricity, this at least proves that there can be exceptions to the validity of the military proposition that 'time spent in reconnaissance is seldom wasted'.

Another near-eccentric was the one who took four chairs and a card table in the car so that the time might be agreeably whiled away should the journey be interrupted by a breakdown. Equally conscious of the need to be prepared for anything was the man who insisted that his chauffeur should never leave him alone in a stationary car in case it should 'bolt'.

Thinking, as well as speaking, of cars in terms of horses was not unusual: there was the peer who would never permit his car to go to the station twice in one day – in case it got tired.

A much stronger claim for inclusion in a list of eccentrics would be that of the Edwardian Duke of Sutherland who was a fine example of a man pursuing a sensible idea to its illogical conclusion. He possessed four Rolls-Royces and insisted that one of them should always be kept ready for instant use. Nobody would disagree that this is a perfectly reasonable idea. Indeed many owners were not considered in the least eccentric if they gave orders that a car should be kept fully maintained with enough petrol in the tank to take in on a long journey at a moment's notice. But the mark of the true eccentric is not so much his pursuit of the logical conclusion, but his failure to stop when he has reached it. This Duke was not content with all the usual precautions. To him 'instant readiness' meant exactly that. There was not a second during any twenty-four hours when the Rolls-Royce selected for that day's duty was not held poised, with its engine running.

There was also an employer who liked always to drive himself, and yet when he drove forth he was invariably accompanied by his chauffeur ensconced in the back. The chauffeur was ready, at the appropriate signal of a raised hand, to turn up the collar of his employer's coat or slip a cushion behind his back, according to the number of fingers stretched out.

A young executive was intrigued by something he noticed when the chairman of the company took him out to lunch. When they came out of the restaurant the chauffeur was sitting at the wheel of the Rolls-Royce. He dismounted and walked round the back of the car to the near-side and opened the door – exactly as the young executive would have expected. However, he noticed that on the way the chauffeur unlatched the rear door on the other side, leaving it slightly ajar. He put it down to a momentary aberration on the chauffeur's part and thought no more about it. But next time he lunched with the chairman the same thing happened again, and in fact every time he entered the car after the chairman he noticed that the door on the opposite side of the car was slightly open. In the end he asked the chauffeur why. The answer was that one snowy day the chairman had slipped as he got into the car, and had fallen forward striking his head on the window-winder opposite. From that day on he insisted that if he should again stumble the door would open at a touch and not give him another bang on the head.

But, with the honourable exception of the gentleman who travelled in the hearse sitting up instead of in the more normal recumbent position, none of these eccentrics reached the sublime heights of surrealist logical looniness of the two spinsters with the 1928 Buick, the dog and the chauffeur called Harold. Every afternoon they liked to go for a drive. Many ladies did that, and it was in no way remarkable. Equally unexceptionable was their dislike of motoring in wet weather.

But there the comparison with ordinary people ceases. Ordinary people would either put up with the rain or sacrifice their daily drive. These ladies did neither.

What they did do was to embark on a glorious charade, scooping up into the chariot of fantasy not only Harold but the dog as well. First of all Harold would jack up both back wheels of the Buick. When this was done the ladies would emerge from the house, dressed in their outdoor clothes, and with the dog on the lead. Harold would be standing waiting with the rear door of the car open and a rug folded over his arm. The ladies would enter the garage and step into the Buick, settling the dog on the seat between them. Harold would tuck the rug round their knees, close the door, and take his own place behind the wheel.

But that was only the beginning. Next he would start up the engine and go through the motions of driving off – first gear, second, top, accelerating until the speedometer showed thirty miles per hour. To make it more interesting he would occasionally toot the horn or make a hand signal. He might change down, as if for a hill, or pretend to pull out to overtake something.

Sometimes, if the afternoon turned out fine after all, they might have a picnic, and Harold would be instructed to take the dog 'to water the trees', solemnly parading round the garage with the animal on the lead. Fortunately the garage was spacious, otherwise they must all have been asphyxiated. Though no doubt if anybody had pointed out to them that not only were they running that danger but that they experienced no changing view of the countryside, they would have looked wide-eyed at him and gently pointed out that it was so much smoother to take a drive without leaving the garage.

Harold did not mind. It was much easier, when he cleaned the car after every outing, to remove the small amount of dust that had gathered in the garage than the mud he would have picked up on the road.

22

Golden Twilight

The 1930s were the last decade in which the future of the private chauffeur looked secure. In those days a young man could start out as a chauffeur confident that there would always be a demand for his services in his chosen career. When the Kenchington brothers went in 1930 to work for Captain Smith-Bingham at Wykham Park near Banbury, the Second World War was nine years off and not yet even a tiny cloud on the distant horizon.

The Smith-Bingham estate of two thousand acres was not considered anything out of the way at a time when an owner of a small manor would be known as a 'thousand-acre man' – a condescending way of implying that he was not really important enough to influence events in his county. Even though the Smith-Bingham estate was not more than just a nice size, the way of life on it, as recalled by Leslie Kenchington, has a dreamlike quality about it.

'We were always very busy, often working until ten o'clock at night, but there was no grumbling, and we all worked as a team. Life there was really a great game, and we always took part in everything, the fishing in Scotland, rough shooting at Wykham and cricket matches in the summer. We had our own staff team and played the neighbouring villages and teams from other estates.

'Once a year there would be the Family Festival Match, which entailed a luncheon and a bar for refreshments afterwards. This was all laid on by Captain Smith-Bingham, and as he was our team captain nothing was spared to make a successful day of it.

'Among the winter activities there would be a Staff Ball, to which surrounding estates' staffs would be invited. The gathering was always in the region of two hundred people and was one hell of a night out.'

Although people who kept a large staff took it for granted that they would employ at least one chauffeur, times were changing. In the 1930s a generation had grown up whose members almost automatically learned to drive. Service stations were more plentiful, cars more reliable and maintenance much reduced. It was, therefore, perfectly feasible for, say, a doctor or a clergyman to dispense with the services of a chauffeur.

In January 1903 Captain Kenneth Campbell DSO read to the 'Automobile Club' a paper entitled 'Motors for Men of Moderate Means'. Amongst the expenses he listed was the cost of employing a 'motor groom', but thirty years later men of moderate means were grooming their own motors. This is not to say that there were fewer chauffeurs, simply that the number of chauffeurs was not increasing at the same rate as the number of cars on the road. From having been almost a necessary concomitant of a car, the chauffeur had become something of a luxury. The sort of people who had previously decided against owning a car on the grounds that to the outlay on the car itself and the running of it must be added the cost of keeping a chauffeur, thus making the whole idea too expensive, now often decided that they could easily cope with driving and looking after a car themselves. The chauffeur was by no means eclipsed, but the star of the owner-driver was rising.

Of course there were still a great many people who, although perfectly capable of driving themselves, found it convenient to employ a chauffeur. All the Royal Dukes, for instance, were keen drivers, yet they all employed chauffeurs. While King George V never drove himself, his sons often did, and the Duke of Gloucester very seldom relinquished the driving seat to his chauffeur, William Prater, who was with him for forty years. The Prince of Wales (later Duke of Windsor) took a keen interest in cars and was a frequent visitor to the mews where the cars of his brother, the Duke of Kent, were garaged. The Prince was always welcome, not least because he always remembered to bring a bag of sweets for the chauffeur's children. The Duke employed two chauffeurs, by name Field and Clarke, and he had at least two particularly interesting cars. In those days the width of a car's body did not extend beyond the chassis members, and the wings which projected to cover the wheels were joined by a running board, which not only protected the body against mud thrown up by the front wheels, but also acted as a step. The Duke of Kent was well aware that when a royal car was moving slowly in procession it was an easy target for an assassin –as had been shown at Sarajevo and Marseilles – and so as not to make things too easy he had his own cars constructed without a running board for a murderer to jump on to. It was not much of a protection, but it was something.

The consequence was that his Rolls-Royces, which bore the distinctive number YR 11, looked exceptionally long and sleek. So did the 4¼ Bentley AXL 1, a black car with four windows and its rear quarters fashionably covered in leather. This body, built by Hooper, had a glass partition, which was extremely unusual, if not unique, for a car with as little room behind the bonnet as the Bentley.

The car was sold after the Duke's death, and it is a measure of how greatly a chauffeur's operating environment had improved since the days when he braved the elements in an open-fronted limousine that, with its partition sealing off the driving compartment and making it snug, the new owner always travelled beside the chauffeur because the engine quickly warmed the front compartment, while the heaterless rear remained icy.

During the 1930s the Prince of Wales's chauffeur was Harry Ladbrook, a large and jolly man whose discretion was taxed to the utmost during the run-up to the Abdication Crisis. While still Prince of Wales the Prince ordered a very special Buick which was built for him in Canada. The standard long chassis limousine was modified so that the occasional seats gave way to an elaborate arrangement of travelling picnic equipment, and the rear quarters were blanked in and their windows replaced with mirrors and reading lights. For the sake of privacy the wide back window was reduced almost to a slit, and when reversing the car Ladbrook had to rely on the mirrors mounted on the spare wheels housed in each front wing.

King George V died before the car was delivered, so that it was as King that Edward VIII first rode in this sumptuous vehicle. Simultaneously there was delivered to Mrs Simpson a very similar Buick. It was dark blue in contrast to the King's black one, and it was on the shorter chassis, but it had the same distinctive modifications, and unless the cars were seen side by side – as they often were – it was very difficult to tell them apart. Ladbrook soon found that his secret was shared with nearly every chauffeur in London.

He did not accompany the Duke of Windsor abroad, and found it impossible to get another job as a chauffeur. This was not because of any lack of skill or experience, in fact rather the reverse. As he confided to another chauffeur, 'No one wants you when you leave royal service. They think you're too good for them and that you'd criticize too much.' Happily, he ended up as doorman at the Coq d'Or restaurant where, clad in a uniform much more resplendent than his previous one, he often saw many of his old friends.

Ladbrook's case was, of course, a special one, and by no means typical for, right up until the outbreak of the Second World War in 1939, there was a steady demand for chauffeurs, particularly as many of these whose careers had started in the early days of motoring had reached retirement age. Not unnaturally, they looked askance at the new generation of young men, who might know all about opening doors and were not too bad at cleaning cars, but who had never taken a gearbox to pieces and put it together again at the roadside.

After the war chauffeuring, like so much else, would never be the same again, and in fact the period covered by the heyday of chauffeuring lasted less than forty years. It was, therefore, perfectly possible and indeed not unusual for a man to become a chauffeur as soon as he was old enough, to serve the same family all his working life, and not to be replaced when he retired.

Such a one was Walter Smith, whose career is recalled with affection by Mrs Marlowe, grand-daughter of his first employer. His elder brother was a coachman, and Walter entered the service of the same employer. He was sent to the Austin works, where he received a thorough training and was taught to drive. This was before the First World War, and by the time Mrs Marlowe remembers him he had come to serve the next generation. This is how she describes him.

'A true gentleman is a cliché, but the only apt description; loyal, kindly, a devoted servant to whom giving service cheerfully was as natural as breathing. In no way subservient, he never dreamed of taking advantage of the fact that he was our friend. In all the years I knew him – and when my Mother died in 1961 he had been with our family for almost fifty years – I never saw him ruffled or anything other than courteous to everyone with whom he came in contact, high or low.'

He was excellent at the little refinements which an intelligent chauffeur developed to do his own job just that little better than others did theirs. He could always be relied on to be at the door of the theatre, or the shop, however many other cars might be queuing up behind him. He took an immense pride in keeping the cars immaculate, and he had spent many hours discovering and perfecting quick routes through London, which became known in 'The Family' as 'Smith's short cuts'. He did not like letting the precious cars out of his sight, and would only consent to them going to a service station for very major overhauls. All such things as decarbonizing he did himself.

'Across the years,' Mrs Marlowe's recollection continues, 'I see him clearly fetching me from boarding school, collecting me from parties, as pleased to see me as I was to see him. Always smiling, and always as impeccably smart as the waiting car.'

Smith was fond of relating a story to illustrate the unselfishness of his employer, to whome he was devoted. During the General Strike of 1926 Smith was driving him home from the City one evening when they saw a long queue of people waiting for some sort of transport to take them home, transport which was unlikely to be forthcoming. Smith was told to stop the car and to cram in as many as it would hold and deliver them to their homes. When it was quite full Smith turned to his employer and said, 'But you haven't left room for yourself, sir.'

'Oh, I'll walk home,' was the reply. This incident happened in Portland Place and 'The Family' lived in Hampstead Garden suburb, a long and uphill walk away.

Smith integrated himself into the life of 'The Family' in the way that many of his generation of servants did. He married a housemaid employed by them, and, very keen on his own garden, he insisted on arranging the flowers in the house for them. He never completely retired while Mrs Marlowe's mother was alive, but would come over from the house which he had bought near their country home in Sussex and do the shopping for her. When, after her death, he came to visit Mrs Marlowe and her husband, he insisted on pruning the roses, and spent hours talking over old times with Mrs Marlowe and the Nanny who lived with her. Both those old servants had known her since birth.

Smith's elder daughter became an architect, and the younger one married a parson who conducted the funeral service when Mrs Smith died. Mrs Marlowe drove over from Hampshire to Sussex for this funeral, and thinking that Smith would appreciate her being suitably dressed, she stopped in Winchester on the way and bought a black hat.

After the service the old man, overcome with emotion, stood holding both her hands outside the church. At first he could not speak, and she waited patiently. Then at last he gulped back his tears and the old familiar smile appeared as he told her, 'I don't like that hat. It makes you look too old.'

23

Turning a Dishonest Penny

It is impossible to imagine Walter Smith or the many loyal and faithful chauffeurs like him cheating their employers. There is, however, ample evidence to show that among chauffeurs as a whole dishonesty was widespread. More than any other servant, the chauffeur had the opportunity to line his own pocket at his employer's expense.

Unless the employer stood over the chauffeur every time he bought a gallon of petrol, a tyre, a sparking plug or a tin of polish, he could not be certain that he was not being cheated. A common trick was simply to tell an employer that something needed to be replaced when in fact it did not. The chauffeur would then sell the new part and carry on using the old one.

Some of this fiddling needed the co-operation of a garage-owner or employee – a faked receipt was valuable to the buyer and the seller – and most of them were ready to comply. In some cases quite major overhauls would be charged for when actually little work had been done.

These practices were downright dishonest, but there was also a whole 'grey area' relating to commission. A garage proprietor was often willing to slip a 'backhander' to a chauffeur without inflating the customer's bill. This was sometimes known to the customer, who regarded it as a legitimate commission for his chauffeur and did not object as long as he was happy that the garage was giving him good service. The garage proprietor was not unduly worried, provided that the chauffeur did not become too greedy. It was a dangerous practice, open to abuse, but when everybody exercised moderation no great harm was done.

The commission on a new car was a different matter. The showroom selling the car had to be prepared to set aside a sum for the chauffeur, and inevitably it was the customer who paid, because he received a smaller amount for his old car in part exchange than he would have done if the firm selling the car had not reserved the 'sweetener' for the chauffeur. This custom was so general that many employers of chauffeurs understood what was happening. Some of them even approved, because it was an encouragement to the chauffeur to see that the car gave good service. This was especially the case when the chauffeur had recommended either the make of the car or the agents selling it in the first place. When given the responsibility he exercised the power that went with it. The employer did have a certain safeguard in that his chauffeur would be unlikely to recommend an unsuitable car, because not only would he be blamed if he did, but also he had to drive and look after it.

Iniquitous though the system of commission was, it worked tolerably well. A chauffeur, having recommended a car, was unlikely to complain about it but one who had not received a commission had no such inhibitions. In the 1930s the London service station of a foreign make had endless trouble with a car belonging to a foreign ambassador. It had been ordered in his own country and shipped through the service station. This firm had not sold the car to the ambassador and so there was no automatic machinery for giving the chauffeur a 'present'. Nobody thought about it – nobody, that is, except the chauffeur.

After a few weeks the car developed an annoying rattle. The ambassador complained to the chauffeur, who protested that from where he sat in front he could not hear it. The ambassador telephoned the service station and asked what he had better do about it. The manager of the service station suggested that the chauffeur should bring the car in to him and he would himself ride in the back, locate the rattle, and have it cured.

The chauffeur duly took the car to the service station and took the manager out in it. Neither of them heard any rattle, and the manager reported to the ambassador accordingly. However, next time the ambassador went out in the car he heard the rattle as loudly as ever. He sent the car back again. After the second visit it was still no better and the ambassador was exasperated. A stinging letter was despatched to the manufacturers telling them that their London agents were useless. The manufacturers threatened to withdraw their agency from the London firm, and the affair took on international overtones. The managing director of the London firm became frantic at the thought of losing this profitable agency; the service station manager, threatened in turn, became frantic at the thought of losing his job; the ambassador became frantic at the thought of having to go on listening to the infuriating rattle. The only person who remained unruffled by the affair was the chauffeur himself.

Finally the works foreman hit upon the solution. He could, he told the service station manager, settle the whole matter for ten pounds. The manager thankfully agreed, the rattle was cured and the ambassador withdrew his complaints. The managing director, curious to know how this happy outcome had been achieved, sent for the foreman and asked him.

'With soft soap,' the foreman replied.

The managing director was incredulous. 'Soft soap? Surely a rattle as persistent as that couldn't be cured with soft soap? Anyway, what part of the car did you apply it to?'

'To the chauffeur's palm.'

It was, of course, the chauffeur who cured the rattle. This was easy for him, for it was he who had created it in the first place. Before taking the ambassador out in the car he had been in the habit of placing a cylindrical tin in the boot with three or four stones in it. Before taking the car to the service station he removed the tin.

Human nature being what it is, skating round the edges of the law was not the sole prerogative of employees. Employers, too, have been known to slip over the dividing line. Gentle blackmail was it appears, the favourite form of chauffeurs' transgression whereas it was the attractions of smuggling which many employers found irresistible. A chauffeur relates an incident at Boulogne. He was waiting in the queue to board the ferry and strolled down the line looking at the parked cars. One of them was a new and beautiful 8-litre Bentley, one of the last of 'WO's' very expensive creations. Behind it was the lady who owned it, hastily rolling on a couple of extra pairs of silk stockings in the hope of saving herself a few pennies Customs duty.

A rather more serious attempt to defraud the Customs involved a chauffeur as an unwitting accomplice. A few weeks after he was engaged by an American who had only recently come to England, they drove together to Liverpool to meet the American's wife, who had travelled from the States on a liner. When she disembarked she got into the waiting Rolls-Royce without even glancing at the chauffeur, whom she had never seen before.

He thought she looked anguished, but it was no concern of his. He was walking round the car to get into the driving seat when the American handed him some documents. 'I'll drive my wife back to London,' he said. 'You bring her car, they're unloading it now. Take it easy, it's brand new.' Then he drove away.

The chauffeur retrieved the car, a Plymouth roadster, and drove it slowly home, running it in carefully. A day after his return his employer came into the garage and told the chauffeur to unscrew the panel supporting the back of the bench seat. Seventy boxes of Havana cigars fell out.

The American, his face expressionless, looked him straight in the eye. 'Well, well,' he said lightly. 'It looks as if my friends back home have sent me a little present.'

These were not isolated incidents, but except in a very few cases chauffeurs were not involved in major crimes. Some of them had to find new jobs in a hurry when their employers were arrested for embezzlement; one or two of them acted as 'inside men' in burglaries. The one who acquired his employer's Rolls-Royce during the employer's lifetime did so quite legitimately. No sensational robbery was involved, and the chauffeur continued in the same employment afterwards.

What happened was this. The employer was a race-horse owner and the chauffeur, whose name was Miller, was affectionately known as 'Dusty'. He was not good at picking winners on the horse-racing courses, but had tremendous luck with the dogs. One day, driving the Rolls-Royce to a race-meeting, he boasted to his employer of his winnings on the dogs the previous evening. The employer pulled his leg a little, ending up with, 'I'll bet you lose all your winnings on the horses today.'

The word 'bet' was a challenge, and Dusty's reply was swift.

'What'll you bet, sir?'

'Your fifty quid to my Rolls-Royce,' was the prompt reply.

The passengers in the car were horrified at the idea of the employer taking fifty pounds off his servant, and they immediately rallied round and offered to cover Dusty's fifty pounds if he lost the bet. 'So he was,' said his employer, telling the story afterwards, 'on a Rolls-Royce to nothing.'

Dusty's luck was in, and he had a marvellous day, picking winners right and left. A true gambler, the employer handed over the car without the slightest demur and immediately went out and bought himself another one. As the first one had been nearly new his wife was surprised to find it replaced and when he sheepishly explained why she was indignantly incredulous.

A short time later, on Dusty's day off, it so happened that the two cars drew up side by side at the traffic lights. Dusty, with the impeccable manners of the respectful chauffeur, inclined his head and gestured with his hand to give his employer the right of way.

But if chauffeurs did not steal cars or drive get-away vehicles in smash-and-grab raids they did sometimes become involved as victims, or potential victims, of crimes associated with motoring. In the very early years of the twentieth century a chauffeur was standing guard over a broken-down car after his employer had gone off in search of a horse to tow it home. It was in the New Forest, miles from anywhere and beginning to get dark when a tramp, carrying a thick club, emerged from the shadow of the trees and demanded money and valuables. The chauffeur, a Boer War veteran, plunged his hand in his coat pocket and grasped the bowl of his pipe, pointing the stem towards the tramp.

'You don't think I'd be by myself in a lonely spot like this if I wasn't armed, do you?' he said. The tramp shambled quickly away.

In the 1930s a modernized type of highwayman appeared in the form of 'car bandits'. They used to park a car or a lorry on a deserted stretch of road and wait until a motorist came along. One of the bandits would then stand in the road waving his arms, effectively blocking the passage of the oncoming car, which had to come to a halt. When it did the other bandits would appear and rob the occupants of the car, usually finishing by deflating one or two tyres so that they could not be pursued. These hold-ups became so prevalent for a time that many chauffeurs used to carry a big spanner or jack handle on the seat beside them.

But this form of hold-up was short-lived. Motorists got wise to it, and refused to stop so that the bandit, jumping for his life, was more at risk than they were. As traffic increased, and as the police in their fast cars became more plentiful as well as more highly trained as drivers, banditry died away.

Many a young chauffeur dreamed of one day having the thrill of being commandeered by a policeman with the order 'follow that car' and tearing through the West End of London in pursuit of an escaping gang.

Sadly, this did not happen often, if ever, and there are no stories of chauffeurs at the wheels of Austin landaulettes or Lanchester limousines hurtling down Piccadilly with horns blaring and lights blazing until they triumphantly overtook escaping criminals and brought them to justice.

Nevertheless there was a documented case of a chauffeur playing a leading role in the apprehension of a gang of wages-snatchers as early as 1909. But, instead of the command 'follow that car', the policeman who leaped aboard the car in Tottenham shouted 'Follow that tram!' The gang (in those days they were known as 'desperadoes') had, after making their wages-snatch at gunpoint, hopped on a passing milkfloat, and only when they were in danger of being caught by the pursuing policeman did they transfer to the swifter vehicle. It must have been a terrifying sight, the hi-jacked tram, its petrified driver with a gun in his back ringing his bell like mad, and the desperadoes spraying the neighbourhood with gunshot.

But although it sounds like a Laurel and Hardy film, it was deadly earnest. Literally deadly, because ten or eleven people died in the carnage. With extreme gallantry the chauffeur braved the bullets and drove his car in front of the tram, blocking its track, whereupon the desperadoes, still spraying bullets, jumped down and ran off. They tried to escape across the Lea Valley marshes, but they were cornered by the indomitable policeman, who grabbed a twelve-bore gun from a startled wildfowler and overcame them when they ran out of ammunition.

For the most part chauffeurs' involvement with capital crimes was at one remove, like the one who lived in Harley Mews and, awaking one night with raging toothache, was skilfully and successfully treated by the nearest doctor and his devoted nurse, a couple of whom the chauffeur could not speak too highly. They were Dr Crippen and Ethel Le Neve.

There were, however, at least three chauffeurs who were convicted of murder. One was hanged; another was sentenced and reprieved. Having completed his sentence he is now living quietly in retirement, all passion spent. The third was employed by Arthur Sutton, of seed fame. This chauffeur developed a practice of advertising for female domestic staff, and meeting them in Mr Sutton's car at the local station. He told them that he was going to drive them to be interviewed by their prospective employer, and then took them into a lonely wood and murdered them. He was eventually caught and hanged.

We are indebted for this story to Mr Sutton's niece, and she tells us that, quite understandably, it took a long time for her aunt and uncle to get over the shock. Her letter concludes, 'Whether they ever employed another chauffeur I do not know.'

24

James across the World

In the 1930s it was quite common to see a car with a GB-plate on the Continent of Europe, and nearly always such a car would be accompanied by a chauffeur. The reason is that most owners of large cars employed chauffeurs, whether they drove themselves or not, and it was the large English cars which were taken abroad. The performance of cars fifty years ago was not impressive by modern standards, and although most makes with engine capacities of four litres could reach something in the region of eighty-five miles an hour they took, on average, five seconds longer to accelerate to fifty miles an hour than a modern car of half the engine capacity takes to reach sixty. The performance of smaller cars was quite negligible, and wholly unsuited to long journeys on the Continent.

Road conditions were slow to improve after the pounding they had received in the First World War, and Alpine Passes were formidable obstacles. (Until the coming of tunnels, well after the Second War, some of the main routes between Northern and Southern Europe passed over untarred tracks across the mountains.) Long-distance touring presented problems for chauffeurs, particularly with a fully laden car, which would often have a heavy cabin trunk carried on a rack protruding well behind the back axle. Before air travel became general, luggage was always heavy, and a crocodile dressing-case, with its battery of gold-topped cut-glass bottles, was a considerable weight to carry, even when empty.

But this was still the era of fast and luxurious long-distance trains, and although touring had greatly increased there were still a lot of people who preferred to travel by train to a destination where they would own or rent a villa and stay in one location until it was time to return home.

Consequently the chauffeur of the 1930s, like his Edwardian predecessors, was often entrusted with bringing the car from England and meeting up with his employer again in the South of France or the Italian Riviera. (English tourists had not yet discovered the Costa Brava.)

It says a great deal for the initiative and reliability of the average chauffeur that the majority of them arrived without anything untoward happening to them on the way. One young rascal who quite definitely did not had recently taken a job with Lord Iliffe. He had never been abroad before, and he decided to have a look at Paris on the way. He looked long and saw a very great deal, finally losing what little money he had left at Longchamps. He had to appeal to the Consul for money to buy petrol, and presented every appearance of being what the Foreign Service laconically calls a DBS – 'Distressed British Subject'. (It is a widely held fallacy that Consuls have a fund for this sort of thing. They do not.) When he eventually turned up at the Carlton in Cannes he was even more distressed. Hungry, unshaven, dropping with fatigue (no money for hotel beds) and with the car filthy and the luggage broken into. Fortunately he was recognized by several chauffeurs who had known him in London. They rallied round and cleaned up both him and the car. He was thankful for their help but was not greatly encouraged by the lugubrious view they took of his plight. 'Cor,' said one of them, summing up the opinion of them all, 'you'll be for the chop, mate. That's for sure.'

They clustered round and watched as he slouched off to report to Lord and Lady Iliffe in their suite at the Carlton. He would, they predicted, be out on his ear in five seconds flat.

They were wrong. It was not until an hour and a half later that he emerged, and when he did he was looking quite different. His eye was bright, and there was a spring in his step. He eagerly related what had happened.

He had felt utterly defeated and had poured out a full confession to the Iliffes, sparing none of the hideous details. They were horrified, but not for the reasons he expected. Deeply religious people with a strong sense of responsibility, they felt that the blame was theirs. They should have foreseen what would happen if they exposed an inexperienced youth to the perils of Paris. They forgave him far more readily than they forgave themselves.

By the mid-1930s employers tended to travel to their destinations by car, so people like the Iliffes were able to keep an eye on chauffeurs likely to get into mischief. Trains were becoming crowded, roads were better and so were cars. It was, therefore, more agreeable to take a leisurely car journey through beautiful and unknown countryside rather than to reach one's destination after an undignified scuffle for a seat on a train.

But if English chauffeurs frequently visited foreign countries with their employers, it was rare for them to take permanent employment abroad. It may be that there was no great demand for them, for English chauffeurs never achieved the international reputation of English butlers. To employ an English butler conferred a tremendous *cachet*, but the same glamour did not accrue to English chauffeurs.

This was probably partly due to the fact that in the very early days it was considered preferable, even in England itself, to have a foreign chauffeur like Evelyn Ellis's French coachman or Captain Knight's Nigerian, very smart in a buff-coloured uniform with red facings. No doubt, too, it was partly due to the fact that mechanical expertise is not a British prerogative. Arabs and Indians, for instance, are extremely clever at keeping machinery running long after its expectation of life has expired.

An even more cogent reason was that in Moslem countries it was considered wrong for a lady to be alone in a car with a man, and the only way round this was to employ a eunuch as chauffeur. Few English chauffeurs possessed this qualification – or lack of qualification, depending on which way you look at it.

Another consideration was that for an expatriate Englishman it was wiser to employ a local chauffeur, even though he might have preferred to take one of his own nationality with him. Anybody who has ever had the misfortune to be involved in an accident in a foreign country will know the feeling of helplessness at having to deal with unfamiliar laws in an unfamiliar tongue. This was particularly true in China, and when Gordon Campbell was appointed to a commercial post in Nanking in 1930 he would not have considered for a moment employing an English chauffeur. Nor would he dream of driving himself for the Chinese Nationalists had fairly arbitrary ways of dealing with Europeans who were thought to have committed some misdemeanor.

Accordingly the Campbells employed a Chinese chauffeur. They never actually learned his name, because he liked always to be addressed as 'Kai Chihti' – the Chinese for driver. He had originally been a bus driver, and this experience had given him a great respect for punctuality. The all-important thing was to keep to the timetable and never to be late. This philosophy would have been admirable grounding for a chauffeur if it had not had a second discipline imposed on it, for Kai Chihti graduated from bus driving to being chauffeur to a general in Chiang Kai Shek's Army. Chinese generals were especially autocratic specimens of the breed, accustomed to sweeping all before them, an attitude enthusiastically adopted by Kai Chihti. Coupled with his obsession of never being late, this arrogant insistence on asserting a priority which he was not automatically accorded made him a terrifying driver.

The Campbells' previous post had been at Wuhoo, where, in the absence of all cars and most roads, their journeys had been made by launch or rickshaw. Nanking was a contrast. The huge bustling city was surrounded by a twenty-mile wall with few gates, and traffic tended to be concentrated on the Chung San Road which connected the European and commercial quarters with the waterfront. The Campbells were provided with an old Ford tourer, with brakes long since past their prime and steering of marked indecisiveness. However there was nothing wrong with the robust old engine, and the car would bound down the busy thoroughfare scattering pedestrians like chaff before the wind, with Kai Chihti in supreme command while the terrified Campbells clung to one another in the back.

Passengers were flung about so much in that old Ford that the mica sidescreens, pierced by many an elbow, gave feeble protection against the monsoon. It was finally replaced by a Morris saloon, a car with a smaller engine and a heavier body. Normally chauffeurs are delighted with new cars, but Kai Chihti mourned the passing of the Ford, whose vices and virtues were so much in accord with his own temperament. Try as he would, he could not coax the sedate saloon into the irresponsible behaviour which had earned its predecessor the reputation of being the terror of the Chung San Road. Kai Chihti himself, however, retained enough verve to warrant the continuance of the nickname with the European community, with more accuracy than originality, had dubbed him, that of 'Jehu'.

The inadvisability of a European failing to employ a local chauffeur in Eastern countries was demonstrated by the diplomat in the Philippines who determinedly drove his own car. This so incensed the Filipino chauffeurs that while he was at a party one night they got together and diligently disconnected and rewired wrongly all the electric connections on his car.

A local chauffeur, of course, was always familiar with local conditions and could conduct himself accordingly, like the one in Corsica in the 1920s who armed himself with a whip for cracking at dogs sleeping in the village streets and a revolver for cracking at bandits. He was also careful not to wear a uniform, for a uniform might be taken to indicate a Government official, and no self-respecting Corsican could resist taking a pot shot at a Government official.

Equally bandit-ridden was Poland immediately after the Second World War in the hiatus between the end of military rule and the establishment of civilian law and order. A family who had survived the various occupations of that unhappy country owed their survival to their chauffeur Wojcik. He had diligently foraged for food for them and also saved them from a burning house. Using petrol left behind by the hurriedly departing German Army, he was one evening driving his elderly employer through a remote forest when the headlights showed the figures of four heavily armed men standing blocking the road. As Wojcik stopped the car they advanced, their guns menacingly pointed at the chauffeur and his employer, and demanded their money and valuables. It so happened that neither man had any money, as the old gentleman had just spent everything on equipment needed to get his factory into production again and was taking his purchases home. He did have, however, a diamond ring and a gold watch which, with the help of Wojcik, he had successfully concealed from the series of looting soldiers who had ravished Poland throughout the war.

Once more Wojcik came to the rescue. Under cover of the darkness he deftly slipped the huge diamond from the old man's finger, grabbed the watch and slipped them both into his mouth. The robbers, unable to believe that a car-owner, displaying an additional sign of opulence in the form of a heavy fur coat, had no money on him, interrogated the old man fiercely. When finally convinced that he really had none, they turned their attention to the chauffeur. Wojcik, with his mouth full, could not speak and his employer interven-ed, explaining, his voice stuttering with fear, that his chauffeur was dumb. Contenting themselves with stealing the belts for the machinery and ripping the fur coat from the old man's back, the bandits made off. Wojcik drove – in silence – for ten kilometres before he deemed it safe to stop. Even then it was several minutes before he had massaged his frozen jaws sufficiently for them to unclamp themselves and disgorge their treasure.

Another East European chauffeur who served his employer as faithfully but quite differently from Wojcik was Vaclav Pecka, the chauffeur to Prince George Christian Lobkowicz, one of the leading Czech racing drivers of the period between the wars. They were both mad about cars, motor cycles, and football, and became inseparable companions, with the Prince financing Pecka's participation in two-wheel events while building up his own car racing career.

The two young men went to Prague together to collect a Type 43 Bugatti which the Prince was giving his sister for a wedding present. They travelled up in another Bugatti and on the return journey the temptation to dice with one another was too strong. The Prince, though victorious, finished up with a much overheated engine in the new car which he ought to have been running in sedately. It took the two of them all night to get the wedding present back in shape for the bride to drive.

After this happy carefree youth it is sad to record that the Prince was killed at the wheel of a racing car, and that Vaclav Pecka lived on until 1975, ending up, after all the terrible things which had happened to Czechoslovakia, as a tractor driver in his native village, which he and the Prince had represented at football so many years before.

A story with a happier ending is that of the Marquis de Dion and his Abyssinian chauffeur Zélélé. They came together at the dawn of the Motor Age and stayed together until the death of the marquis in 1946, his ninety-first year. Zélélé not only drove de Dion Bouton cars in reliability trials, but his smiling shining face appeared in advertisements for them. He became indispensible to the old marquis, who referred to him as his Man Friday.

They remained in Paris throughout the Second World War and when there was a total ban on petrol they resurrected one of the 1889 steam tricycles and carefully saved coal briquettes to fuel it. Then off they went, trundling round Paris with urbane disregard for the feelings of the Occupying Power, while scrupulously observing the letter of the law. The Nazis looked on in baffled fury, suspecting that they were being teased but unable to do anything about it. They never did know how to handle Parisian panache.

When peace and petrol returned to France the two intrepid pioneers made another spectacular appearance, this time in a de Dion vis-à-vis of 1898, in which the old gentlemen sat acknowledging the plaudits of the Press and the cameramen with the aplomb of which age never robbed them.

Just as the grand partnership of the marquis and Zélélé was drawing to its close in Paris, so the career of another distinguished chauffeur was burgeoning on the other side of the Atlantic. The British Mission to the newly-formed United Nations had one of the first post-war Rolls-Royces, and to drive it they engaged George Tambone. Thirty-five years later he was still serving the British Heads of Mission with the devotion and flair with which he had eased the passage of succeeding ambassadors. 'George knew everything and everybody. He could always get you things which you hadn't got time to go searching for yourself,' said one Head of Mission. 'He was one of the family.'

Equally, everybody knew George. Once he spent a holiday in London and joined the little knot of sightseers outside the door of No. 10 Downing Street. At that moment the Prime Minister of the day, Sir Alec Douglas Home, emerged. Catching sight of George he ducked past the police and through the crowd to greet him warmly and shake him by the hand.

George and the Rolls-Royce became famous in New York, and George resisted the only attempt to part him from it. A new Head of Mission remarked that, as he had been appointed by a Labour Government, he thought a less patrician vehicle would be more suitable. George put him in his place with impeccable politeness.

'It might be more suitable for you, sir. But we often carry Prime Ministers and Foreign Secretaries in this car. For them, nothing else would be appropriate.'

It would be nice to record that the car served George as faithfully as he served it. But on one memorable occasion it let him down as badly as it could. While conveying no less a personage than the Right Honourable Harold Macmillan it chose to break down in the tunnel running under the East River. Probably in the whole history of motoring no chauffeur has ever found himself in such a humiliating position. Responsible for the Rolls-Royce, that symbol of the quiet good taste of British superiority, there he was, stuck in the tunnel with traffic building up all round him, while sitting in the back was the man who had just electrified the Assembly of the United Nations with a scintillating exhibition of British leadership. George got out and pushed.

Throughout the whole hideous drama the Prime Minister sat happily chatting to his companion, rising splendidly above the embarrassment and showing yet again how right the world's Press had been to dub him 'unflappable'. Such was the calibre of both Harold Macmillan and George Tambone that the incident soon faded into obscurity and George's reputation did not suffer. The British Mission remained the envy of the nations of the world. No other Mission could find a chauffeur to equal George.

An infinitely more humble chauffeur is, nevertheless, worthy of respect for having produced what must be the absolutely perfect answer to turn away an employer's wrath. So low down did he come in the hierarchy of chauffeurs that he did not even have a uniform and was only allowed to drive the 'shopping car'. His employer, a Texan, ordered a new Lincoln and it was delivered on the day before he was leaving for a trip to Europe.

'Douglas, while I'm away you are on no account to touch that car. On no account at all. Is that quite clear?'

Douglas eagerly affirmed that it was. Nothing would induce him to go near it, he vowed.

Of course as soon as his employer was safely on the plane Douglas took the car out for an airing. A bee flew into his eye and he drove the Lincoln into a wall, demolishing both it and the car.

'I distinctly told you not to touch it. You understood my orders. Why did you disobey me, Douglas? Why?' The employer glared at him when Douglas mutely opened the garage door and disclosed the remains.

Douglas spread his hands in a helpless gesture and shook his head sorrowfully. 'Well suh,' he said, 'I guess dat ole' Debble jus' entered into me.'

25

James on the Screen

Real chauffeurs were scarce in Hollywood in the Golden Age of Motoring. There were glamorous cars and glamorous stars, but the chauffeur was not much seen. The reason was that driving an exotic car was considered a symbol of virility and an ageing star would as soon be driven by a chauffeur as he would be pushed in a wheelchair.

On the screen, of course, it was quite a different matter. Chauffeurs were portrayed whenever either the plot demanded it or it was necessary to imply luxury. The plot was often helped along by somebody playing the part of a character masquerading as a chauffeur, such as Brian Aherne in *Merrily We live* (1938) or François Perier in Cocteau's *Orphee* (1949). The masquerading might have some subtle significance: a spy planted to overhear secrets, perhaps, or a gangster luring an unsuspected victim to his fate. Or it might be, as in the Aherne picture, the good old comedy formula of mistaken identity. In this film he is a roving writer, and calls at Billie Burke's sumptuous home in order to ask to use her telephone. But she mistakes him for a tramp and before he can disabuse her she gives him a meal and engages him as chauffeur. Fitted up with uniform, he is despatched to the station to collect her husband on his return from the City.

When Aherne arrives at the station he is amazed to see a long line of limousines, each with its attendant chauffeur awaiting his employer. All the cars look the same, so do the chauffeurs, and Aherne attempts to slot himself into this unfamiliar scene, standing with a foot nonchalantly resting on the bumper. The train arrives, the chauffeurs spring to open doors, and Aherne suddenly realizes that he has no idea what his new employer looks like. Accordingly he strides up and down the platform bawling, 'Mister Kilbourne, Mister Kilbourne.' He is pursued by a mousy little man, beautifully played by Clarence Kolb, dodging between the alighting passengers. Finally he catches up with Aherne and says very quietly, 'Will you stop shouting my name, you fool, and drive me home.'

This was no means the only film to portray unchauffeurlike behaviour. In *Night Nurse* Clark Gable was shown giving Barbara Stanwyck a terrific sock on the jaw while she is playing a nurse baby-sitting. 'Who are you?' she demands, eyes wide with fear. The camera shows Gable's grim face as he growls through gritted teeth, 'I'm Nick the Chauffeur.'

But if, in real life, Nick would have found it difficult to get a job with the sort of references he deserved, an employer would have had to be absolutely mad to take on the chauffeur portrayed by Robert Shaw in *The Hireling*. His behaviour was even more unbecoming to a chauffeur than was Nick's, for, in desperate drunken frustration, he savagely attacked his own Rolls-Royce. What had driven him to these lengths was his passion – unrequited – for the young widow who hired his car to drive her round the countryside in an effort to come to terms with her husband's death.

Another film in which a chauffeur played a role of high drama was *Night of the Generals* (1966), with Tom Courtenay as chauffeur to Peter O'Toole.

But of all the dramas in which chauffeurs have appeared the most arresting must be *Sunset Boulevard* (1950) for it bore a chilling resemblance to the careers of its stars, Gloria Swanson and Erich von Stroheim, both of whom were by then past their zeniths. Miss Swanson had been Cecil B. deMille's hottest property, and von Stroheim had actually directed her in a film, never completed, called *Queen Kelly*. In *Sunset Boulevard* she plays a filmstar in decline, with Erich von Stroheim as her general factotum, who has himself seen better days as a great Hollywood personality. One day there comes a telephone call from Cecil B. deMille himself, asking her to come to the studios. Electrified with dreams of a comeback, this character summonses her faithful chauffeur and he wheels out the once-famous car. Off they go, driving right into the Paramount backlot where they are greeted by Cecil B. deMille.

Then comes the terrible truth. It was, he tells her, not her and her chauffeur that he wanted, but her car. The shock is so great that soon she goes mad, kills the man who has misled her, and then tries to kill herself, finally making her last 'entrance' for the benefit of the newsreel cameras which have gathered to record her arrest.

After all this harrowing verisimilitude, it is a relief to be able to record that with this film the 53-year-old Gloria Swanson and von Stroheim scored a resounding success.

But, by and large, Hollywood films use chauffeurs rather like stage 'props' to indicate that the employer is rich. If the chauffeur just sits there looking wooden, that is enough. An early use of this formula was in 1925, when Pola Negri dazzled the silver screen in *Woman of the World*. Eight years later a chauffeur-driven limousine was used for Joan Crawford's entrance in *Dancing Lady* (1933), and John Indrisano performed the same service for Mae West in *Go West Young Man* (1936). Ingrid Bergman, too, plays a woman making a sensational entry into a small town, with a chauffeur-driven car to underline how rich she is (*The Visit*, 1964).

And, of course, there was one film which, without a chauffeur, would have been as pointless as Hamlet without the Prince – *The Yellow Rolls-Royce*, mainly driven by Richard Pearson, though at some stages of the plot the car is owner-driven by Miss Bergman.

A star who twice played the part of a chauffeur was Cary Grant, in *Sinners in the Sun* (1932) and *Romance and Riches* (1936).

But the chauffeur's steadiest contribution to Hollywood was in comedy. Orson Welles used a fleet of chauffeur-driven limousines to make the satirical point of world-weary millionaires being taken across a sandy beach to a picnic in *Citizen Kane* (1941), and the Marx Brothers used broader satire in *Duck Soup* (1933). But as the joke hinged on Harpo and Groucho changing places in the driving seat, which was in any case a motorcycle saddle, they hardly qualify as playing chauffeurs within the definition of the word.

A perennial Hollywood convention was first introduced by Buster Keaton in *The Navigator* (1924). He gives an address to his driver who executes a U-turn and says, 'We're here, sir.' Absurdity always gains a laugh, and this gag has cropped up in at least five other films, and no doubt there will be many more. No doubt, too, film chauffeurs will go on wearing breeches, leggings and tunics buttoned to the neck.

Low-budget English films, instead of buying a limousine for an actor to drive, often hired a car with chauffeur complete. However, on one occasion the director must have realized that he had made a false economy. The sequence was a simple one, merely requiring the

Daimler to be driven up to a front door and to stop. The hero would then leap out and run into the house. This was carefully explained to the chauffeur, an intelligent young man who quickly grasped it all.

He loaded the actor in the back and drove smartly up the drive, bringing the car to a halt at the front door.

'Cut!' shouted the director, who then turned to the chauffeur. 'You're supposed to be in a hurry. Drive faster. Much faster. Right, we'll take it again.'

This time the chauffeur roared up the drive and felt sure that never had a Daimler limousine given such an impression of speed. 'Cut!' shouted the director. 'Hey, you, I said *faster*. *Much* faster.'

The chauffeur protested but the director, by this time very angry, shouted him down.

Once again the chauffeur took the car to the bottom of the drive, turned it and accelerated savagely towards the house. The big car swayed and lurched as he tugged at the wheel and swung it round in front of the house. It looked magnificent but, as the chauffeur had warned, it was faster than practicable. A fierce hail of gravel flew up at the whirling cameras, smashing them all. In the awed silence which followed the only voice to be heard was that of the director.

'Cut!' he shouted, rather unnecessarily in the circumstances.

26
Son of James

By the 1930s the original pioneer chauffeurs had mostly retired or died, but they were usually replaced. It was not until the outbreak of the Second World War that the British way of life changed sufficiently dramatically for chauffeurs to become a rarity.

Typical of many during this period is the history of the Beaulieu chauffeurs. Teddy Stephens died in 1932 and was succeeded by Frank Wallis. Frank had started in the gardens of Palace House, graduated to driving Lady Montagu's pony and trap, then mechanized himself with a lorry before becoming chauffeur. When the widowed Lady Montagu married Captain Edward Pleydell-Bouverie in 1936 he already had a chauffeur-valet, William Martin, and both men were sent to the Rolls-Royce school.

William Martin went to help build power boats at the beginning of the war, and Frank stepped in to help in the house in place of the depleted staff. Butling was not at all to his liking but, like many loyal servants, he adapted himself uncomplainingly to circumstances which had altered so drastically with the coming of the war. As soon as it was over he returned thankfully to his real job of chauffeuring, and remained at it until his death in 1962.

Upon his return from the war factory, William Martin was set up with the Bucklers Hard Garage, which he still runs. Gone were the days when households could employ two or more chauffeurs, and the conditions of employment of even those who could still keep one were now quite different. The Second World War saw the end of chauffeuring as it had been for half a century. It would never be the same again.

It is true that for a few years after the war there were still pre-war cars, pre-war chauffeurs, and pre-war employers like 'Er Upstairs who still slipped an extra pound into her chauffeur's pay packet to test whether he was honest enough to return it, but they all dwindled away with age.

There are, of course, still chauffeurs, but the whole pattern of their employment is quite different from what, it was. The old family chauffeur is rare indeed today. As with other forms of traditional domestic service, it simply does not occur to a young lad that he should become chauffeur to a private employer and remain with him and his descendants all his working life. The door which used to be wide open is now only a narrow slit.

There are two main openings for chauffeurs. To be employed by a company to drive its chairman, or to drive for a hire firm. Driving the chairman of a company is the nearest there is to the old system of family chauffeur, for both chairman and chauffeur regard it as exactly the same, in that the chauffeur takes orders and the chairman gives them as if he were the actual employer. On the other hand there are several important differences. When the chairman retires the chauffeur will not move with him, or be passed on to the next generation of the family. He will remain in the service of the same employer – the company – although he will be driving the new chairman. The chauffeur no longer has the continuity of the family but he does have continuity of employment, and when he, in his turn, retires, his pension will be paid by the company's own scheme. This can be relied on, but he can no longer expect the sort of windfall which long-service chauffeurs often used to receive in the wills of their late employers. No company ever bequeathed a chauffeur his house.

Perhaps the most important difference between a family chauffeur and one employed by a company is that the company chauffeur is automatically entitled to be paid overtime and has generous paid holidays in line with other employees. He usually has weekends to himself. Indeed there is the chairman of one very large company who can often be seen cleaning his own car on Sundays because he would be ashamed to take it to his office on Monday morning and let the company chauffeur see that he would be content to drive about in a dirty car.

The company chauffeur in general is every bit as particular about keeping the car spotless as his predecessors were. One of them was deeply shocked when we suggested to him that he took the Daimler to an automatic carwash. Although the car is kept in a public garage, without the washing facilities there used to be in the old-fashioned mews, he takes it three times a week to a 'manual' carwash where he washes it with a soft sponge and soapy water, then rinses it in cold water. The 'automatic' part comes in to blow it dry, after which the chauffeur finishes it off with a leather. This is typical of chauffeurs driving company chairmen. They still are proud that their cars are just a bit glossier than those next to them in the traffic block. They are very conscious that they do not spend as much time polishing the car as a pre-war chauffeur did, but then they probably spend more time driving it than he did. As one of them put it, 'My employer spends more time in the back of his car than he does in front of his desk.'

As a company employee the chauffeur has a contract of service, and stipulations about cleanliness are usually written into it. Less emphasis is placed on mechanical knowledge than it used to be, largely because service stations nowadays have special equipment with which they can do maintenance work more quickly and efficiently than any man working on his own. A chauffeur is usually required to have sufficient knowledge to keep the car roadworthy, but it is unnecessary for him to be highly technical.

A role which is very much of our time is that of chauffeur to a pop star. Apart from the basic responsibility of getting his employer to and from the right place at the right time he has to fend off the fans and plan ingenious evasive action, so that his task combines that of driver with those of secretary, bodyguard and almost nanny.

The modern chauffeur is probably just as conscientious as his predecessor, but he is working in a changed environment, and he must adapt to it. Chauffeurs still do fill in half an hour when they are waiting by dusting down the car, but the rigid rule of cleaning a car after every journey is almost certainly now confined to the royal mews. There the cars are still cleaned every time they go out, even if it is only from Buckingham Palace to Clarence House.

In a curious way, the chauffeur of the 1980s is closer to the chauffeur of eighty years ago than he is to the one of forty. Like Bernard Shaw's 'New Man' he is an individualist, doing the job because he likes it. And, like the early 'motor experts' he is a specialist who hires out his services and goes home when his day's work is done. For it is rare, certainly in London, for a chauffeur to be provided with accommodation.

Besides driving for a company, the obvious opening for a chauffeur is to work for a hire company. This, however, is not a career which a young man could embark on because when driving 'for hire or reward' insurance companies insist on a minimum age limit of twenty-five. It is the hire companies which buy most of the now limited production of seven-passenger limousines, and the chances are that the great majority of such cars which one sees being driven by chauffeurs do belong to the companies. There are cases of owner-drivers who operate independant car-hire, preferring to be their own masters, but they do not claim to have any financial advantage.

On the whole chauffeurs consider that they are at least adequately paid, which suggests that they probably always did. For while their wages have multiplied by twenty or twenty-five times since before the Second World War the costs of the cars they drive have increased by a like factor.

The attitude towards the job is, in many cases, just as it always was, and the words spoken by a thirty-year-old chauffeur in 1980 might be an echo of sentiments expressed any time these last eighty years. He was a specialized craftsman who had been made redundant. He became a chauffeur because, he said, 'The only other thing I really understood, and liked to do, was to drive a car. I could drive a car for hours and hours and hours on end. Although I do feel tired at the end of a journey, I have enjoyed it. It's a form of recreation to me, a way of expressing myself. It's a pastime, like fishing is to some people or badminton is to others.'

This unchanging fascination with driving will ensure that as long as there are employers there will be chauffeurs eager to be employed. It is the lack of opportunity which has reduced their numbers, not the lack of the wish to be a chauffeur. It is highly unlikely that anyone would answer a question in the way in which an applicant for a commission in the Royal Navy did in the First World War. When, among the general knowledge items, an Admiral asked him, 'What makes a motor car go?' he smartly replied, 'A chauffeur sir.'

Chauffeurs may be a dwindling race. They are certainly not a dying one. Already there are signs that the career of driving an employer's vehicle, a career which made a transition from coachman to chauffeur, will cross a new threshold. We know of cases of the company chauffeur being retrained to pilot the company helicopter.

But even if chauffeuring should disappear altogether, unless human nature undergoes a complete change there will always be men willing to give loyal and faithful service in one form or another; men like William

King, who is commemorated on a headstone in a remote Irish graveyard with these words:

Head Coachman and afterwards Chauffeur at Powerscourt for 43 years.
Died March 22nd 1946.
Erected to his memory by Viscount Powerscourt.